school of
INTENTIONAL
LIVING

Scriptures taken from the Holy Bible, New International Version®, NIV®. Copyright © 1973, 1978, 1984, 2011 by Biblica, Inc.™ Used by permission of Zondervan. All rights reserved worldwide. www.zondervan.com The "NIV" and "New International Version" are trademarks registered in the United States Patent and Trademark Office by Biblica, Inc.™

Scripture quotations marked MSG are taken from *The Message*, copyright © 1993, 2002, 2018 by Eugene H. Peterson. Used by permission of NavPress. All rights reserved. Represented by Tyndale House Publishers.

Scripture quotations marked (TLB) are taken from *The Living Bible*, copyright © 1971 by Tyndale House Foundation. Used by permission of Tyndale House Publishers, Carol Stream, Illinois 60188. All rights reserved.

Dedication

This book is dedicated to all who dare

to shift from survival mode to

living intentionally.

Recommendations

I f you struggle to be consistent and disciplined in your daily walk with Jesus and others, then this book is for you! Elaine Friedrich has given us a true gift with her rich experience, marvelous examples, and thought-provoking things to ponder about living in the grace and power of the Holy Spirit. My faith was strengthened as I gobbled up practical ideas and methods to strengthen every area of my life! Your heart will be encouraged and emboldened to be intentional in all your relationships---with God and others, so that life here and eternally will be abundant!

Dr. Joy Griffin
Founder of Beautiful Feet
Co-founder of International Leadership Institute
Carrolton, GA

For Elaine, "Intentional" is more than a title. "Intentional" is a way of life. Every foundational principle that Elaine shares is rooted in God's Word and then wonderfully connected and applied to our daily lives. Anyone seeking to be a Christ-centered leader in today's world will be offered valuable life resources for themselves and for those they have been called to lead. Elaine wholistically addresses how to truly live a life that matters by giving us truth and tools to encourage us in our spiritual, physical, relational, intellectual, and financial arenas of life. Great book for myself, our family, and our church!

Dr. Andy Hurst
Senior Pastor
St. Luke's Methodist Church
Lubbock, Texas

Dr. Elaine Friedrich's newly published book, *Making Every Day Matter,* is an excellent practical guide to growth as a believer spiritually, physically, relationally, intellectually, and financially. You are given grounded Biblical truths on each topic, with deeper understanding behind why these practices are important to develop in your faith journey. Her "101 ways" provides exceptional practical principles to apply daily to build your faith. This book can be used in a devotional style, or can be applied within a group setting, implementing these principles together as a community of believers.

Amy Wasserbauer, M.Div., Ph.D.
Clinical Psychologist
Renewed Hope Counseling, LLC
Phoenix, Arizona

Forward

L iving in a world full of distractions, demands, and busyness, it is quite easy to lose focus on what exactly matters in life. Dr. Elaine Friedrich's book, *Make Every Day Matter: 101 Ways to Live Intentionally with Purpose, Presence, and Peace*, brings light to any who want to live intentionally and make the most out of their one and only life. Using her vast experience as a church leader, professor, trainer, and coach, Elaine gives the reader 101 practical ideas for developing into better stewards of time, energy, and resources for living a more purposeful life.

The crux of the message of *Make Every Day Matter* is the investment of our personal capital in five major areas of life: spiritual, physical, relational, intellectual, and financial. Each of these facets is important in our life, and together, they contribute to the meaningful and wholistic way of living.

Spiritual capital constitutes the bedrock on which everything else in our lives should be built. Investment in our relationship with God puts us in step with our calling in the kingdom, enabling us to live in authenticity and powerfully change people's lives through living out our faith. We draw strength for the journey ahead through prayer, meditation, and spiritual practices into a deepening relationship with Jesus.

Physical capital insists that the great and due care of our bodies attests to our physical body as temples of the Holy Spirit. By striving for good health, self-care, and physical fitness, we are caring for what God has given to us, having knit us together in our mother's womb. We are challenged to make healthy choices concerning diet, exercise, and rest if we are going to live the life God has called us to, being effective and influential in our relationships and service.

Relational capital brings into focus that there is a need to build up and foster deep and connections with others. As creatures created in the relational image of God, we were called to mirror God's love and compassion in all interactions. By investing time and energy in developing healthy relationships with your family, friends, colleagues, and even strangers, a community develops that sustains, understands, and encourages life to its fullest.

Intellectual capital challenges us to use our minds and talents to develop ourselves by gaining knowledge, wisdom, and personal growth. In doing so—constantly learning, acquiring new skills, and using our gifts in service to others—we expand our horizons, deepen our insights into the world around us, and make significant contributions to serve others. While these latter two traits make life interesting and meaningful for ourselves, intellectual curiosity and creativity enable us to make a positive difference in the lives of others and in the world.

Financial capital completes the more pragmatic part of the stewardship invitation to manage resources with wisdom and generosity. Being thankful that everything we possess is ultimately from God, we can approach all our money with a spirit of gratitude, responsibility, and generosity. A giving heart to the needy, causes which parallel our values, and using our finances to expand God's kingdom. Developing a life of generosity enables us to provide for not only our families but also towards ministries that serve the least, the last, and the lost.

In *Make Every Day Matter*, Dr. Friedrich has painted in broad strokes a roadmap for living more intentionally. She offers practical suggestions and actionable steps to take-and make the needed capital investments in these five key areas of life. By implementing these suggestions into our daily activities and decision-making processes, we make a life truly worth living: one filled with meaning, significance, and making a difference for Jesus.

Dr. Jody Ray
Lead Pastor
Mt. Bethel Church
Marietta, GA

How to Read This Book

As you read *Make Every Day Matter: 101 Ways to Live Intentionally with Purpose, Presence, and Peace*, here are some general guidelines as you read. With its focus on five key areas - Spiritual Capital, Physical Capital, Relational Capital, Intellectual Capital, and Financial Capital - this book provides practical tips and ideas to help you live a more purposeful and fulfilling life.

One thing to keep in mind while reading the book is, of course, that you don't necessarily read it cover to cover. It would be better to focus on an area in your life in which you want to make intentional investments and pick and choose the ideas in that area that most resonate with you.

Whether this is to boost your spiritual life, make your body healthier, enhance relationships, grow in an area of knowledge, or increase your finances, there are 20 ideas under each of those areas to help and direct you. For example, if you want to work on the Spiritual Capital, just go to the section dealing with that particular area and sees different ideas suggested. Don't be in a hurry. It would be better to take your time and be intentional about how this idea might be helpful to live a life more focused on purpose, presence, and peace.

In each of the ideas the actual concept is described. Then it is summarized as the big idea behind it. Included is a Scripture passage for reflection based on the idea presented. Then a practical way to implement the idea into your life is given to help you actually implement it into your life. You may choose to focus on one idea at a time and weave it into your daily routine. The goal is to be more intentional in how you live your life.

If you want to develop and increase the investment of your Physical Capital, go to that section of the book and decide which idea you would want to work on first. You can't implement everything at once. This book is designed to begin to be intentional in each of these five capitals in order to experience life to its fullest.

You can also use this book as a daily or weekly guide apart from focusing on specific areas of your life to stay on course with your intentional investments. Refer to the ideas and concepts housed in this book regularly to remind yourself to live purposefully, be present, and have peace of mind.

You can also use this book as a guide for a small group experience to begin intentionally working on the various aspects of your life in order to keep your life in balance. As you mentor others, this book can be used as a guide to begin conversations stewarding all dimensions of life.

However you use it, it's not meant to breeze through it in order to check it off of your 'books to read' list. Use it to systematically work on making wise choices of your investment of time, energy, and resources.

TABLE OF CONTENTS

Spiritual Capital

This section addresses the nature of investment in spiritual capital and will be explored from the Christian perspective. It is strongly believed that our relationship with God is the foundation of who we are as human beings, and it is that which grants us true value and purpose in life. In nurturing our spiritual growth, focusing on strengthening a relationship with the Lord aligns us to God's divine plan for us and empowers us to live out our faith in a way that positively affects those around us. Unlike the pursuit of material wealth, investing in spiritual capital is the development of inner qualities and virtues that mirror the character of Christ. We can be attentive to God's leading in our lives and learn ways, through spiritual disciplines, that will provide depth and insight to a life that is called to follow Him. In investing time, effort, and resources to the growth of spiritual capital, we are prepared to live authentically, with integrity, and with meaning, reflecting Christ's love into a world in desperate need of hope and light.

#1 Cultivate Spiritual Disciplines

Cultivating the spiritual disciplines is essential for believers to develop a closer relationship with God. By dedicating time to daily Scripture study and prayer, individuals create a sacred space to connect with the Lord and experience spiritual growth. These practices lay the foundation for Christians to navigate the challenges and opportunities that life presents, helping us to align our lives with the words and ways of Jesus. This self-discipline leads to a life of obedience and deepening faith.

The Big Idea

The big idea, as we cultivate spiritual disciplines is that we begin a consistent and persistent practice of engaging with the Lord. As we put these disciplines into practice and prioritizing this time in our daily life, we create a space for intimacy with the Lord. Guided by the Holy Spirit, this focus gives us direction for daily living. The goal of practicing the spiritual disciplines is that we are transformed into the image of Christ.

The Word

Psalm 46:10 *Be still, and know that I am God; I will be exalted among the nations, I will be exalted in the earth.*

Looking at this passage, we see the significance of being still before the Lord. Only in the quiet can we truly hear the voice of God. In our over busy world, we have to intentionally carve out time to be silent. In solitude, we are able to connect with the Father and be present before Him. As we get to know Him, we are able to grow in our relationship with Him and have a posture of humility as we grasp the vastness of His greatness. We then can more fully rest in His sovereignty.

Putting It Into Practice

In order to implement spiritual disciplines in our life, we must control our calendars and set aside time for scripture reading and prayer. Developing the habit of having a time of silence and quietness with the Lord is essential for spiritual growth. Setting aside time either in the morning or right before bed, helps to get into a routine for this practice. Keeping distractions to a minimum is important in order to connect with God. Using a journal will help you to capture insights, prayers, and give you the ability to write down what you hear from God in your quiet time.

#2 Practice Gratitude

For a believer, gratitude is important because it is met with humility and knowing that all that we have is because of God. It gives a broader view of life and shows that all aspects of living are a blessing. Whenever we practice gratitude daily, we inspire and motivate others. Since our faith is grounded in God, through His love and grace, we can attest to that God's power and ability to change our life. On top of that, gratitude helps in recognizing and acknowledging God's provision, reminding one that it is He who provides for us, and our needs are met abundantly. Being conscious of these blessings enables us to be joyful, irrespective of our situations. We focus not on things that we lack but on the things that we have. Through thankfulness, we allow and open ourselves to His grace and blessings; it is in this way that we experience a much deeper level of fulfillment and purpose.

The Big Idea

The big idea of gratitude is that it puts us in a humble disposition, reminding us that all we have is from God. It involves being a witness of our faith and trust in God, regardless of our present circumstances.

The Word

1 Thessalonians 5:18 *Give thanks in all circumstances; for this is God's will for you in Christ Jesus.*

The passage reminds us of God's desire for us as believers: to give thanks in everything. It doesn't say to give thanks 'for everything.' We can thank God when things are easy but this verse challenges us to have an attitude of gratitude even in difficult times. We express our confidence in God's provision and in His sovereignty over our lives when we give thanks in all circumstances. It is in this act of thanksgiving that we are aligned with God's heart, making us open to grace and blessing.

Putting It Into Practice

We can find a way to be grateful every day. Some days may be more difficult but let's prepare for that time by finding a large jar. As you think about things for which you are grateful, jot it down on a slip of paper and put it in your 'Gratitude Jar.' On days when you need to be reminded of things you are grateful for, pull out one or two to read. As your jar fills up with the things you are grateful for, you will be encouraged even in the midst of discouragement. Get your whole family involved by adding to your 'Gratitude Jar.' By developing this attitude of thankfulness, we can encourage and motivate all those people around us with the power of change brought about by a thankful heart.

#3 Look in the Mirror

Self-reflection enables you to look at your thoughts, actions, and motivations for your life. One of my favorite phrases is 'A life without reflection, is a life without direction.' Checking and reflecting on your behaviors and motivations enables you to make choices consistent to your faith and implement changes as needed. Pausing and taking time to evaluate our lives results not only in spiritual growth but in a deepening of our relationship with God. Having a rhythm of reflecting daily or weekly establishes the focus of what really matters to us in our lives.

The Big Idea

Taking time for reflection is the act of stopping and evaluating our thoughts, actions, and motivations especially in the light of God's word. This helps us to take stock on our life and make course corrections as needed. This reflection enables us to focus or refocus on what really is important in our life. By thinking deeply on our life, we are able to give more of ourself to God which brings us closer in our relationship with Jesus.

The Word

Proverbs 27:19 *As water reflects the face, so one's life reflects the heart.*

This verse is a vivid reminder that our life is built on what's in our heart. Exactly like the face can be seen through its reflection, so the state of our heart can be seen easily from our actions, behaviors, and decisions. Self-reflection becomes a needed practice in order to gauge the condition of our heart. This calls us to check, from time to time, on our thoughts, intentions, and actions, that they measure up to the longings of the heart. And when we take a closer look at ourselves in reflective ways, we see discrepancies or places of misalignments where growth usually means change for us. Through close examination, we are able to cultivate a heart reflecting godly values, virtues, and love. It involves the intentional practice of reflection through which we are shaping our character to be like the character of Christ.

Putting It Into Practice

You can incorporate self-reflection into your daily life by setting a specific time each day or week to engage in a personal reflection activity. This is done through first ensuring a place that is quiet, reading scripture, meditating, and journaling. You might sit for thirty minutes each morning for personal reflection about thoughts, actions, and attitudes from the previous day. You can remember conversations you had, experiences you encountered, and reflect. Simple prompts may include: What went well? What did I learn? How might I improve the next time I encounter this situation? Using self-reflection consistently in your life will not only strengthen your relationship with God but will help you to grow in other areas of your life as well.

#4 Sabbath Keeping

We understand and know that we need renewal for our body, soul, and spirit. It is a time to restore and refocus ourselves and our relationship with God. Intentionally, by setting apart this one day to rest, we recognize that our value and our identity isn't grounded how much we can do or how much we can accomplish. Our identity is found in Christ.

Sabbath rest provides a sacred space, a withdrawal from our daily responsibilities, to experience God's presence fully and find comfort in His grace. This deliberate rest will allow us to have time to think about priorities and realign them according to God's design for our life. That gives us a chance to reflect on ourselves, examine our inner selves, and focus on spiritual things. It is in this purposefully created space that we can have all the benefits of Sabbath observance, drawing closer to God and those whom we love. This enables us to feed our souls, refuel, and enter into the rest of the days that follow with renewed vision. Keeping the Sabbath isn't just a spiritual discipline; it's a grace that creates a closer relationship between us, God, and others and by His grace, toward a fuller, more balanced life.

The Big Idea

In Sabbath keeping, what comes into mind is a life that desires to rest, relax, and rejuvenate. Taking one day from the week off from our daily duties and responsibilities, we are consciously setting time aside for strengthening our relationship with the Lord and our loved ones. This practice is not only for God's glory but also for our own sake as individuals. It gives perspective in life and prepares one for the days ahead.

The Word

Exodus 20:8 *Remember the Sabbath day by keeping it holy.*

The passage reminds us that God commanded us to remember the Sabbath day and to keep it holy. In other words, set apart one day in the week just for God's sake. It is the day put to honor Him and rest our bodies. Keeping the Sabbath is, therefore, a confession of God as Creator over all things, even time, and our being subject to His design for our good. The invitation here is divine: into rest, restoration, and realignment of our priorities for the work that God has called us to do.

Putting It Into Practice

This is a tough one to incorporate into our life in our present day. By being intentional and creative in making the practice of Sabbath-keeping part of the weekly routine, we find rest. You might choose to set every Sunday or Saturday aside as a Sabbath day on which you don't work at all or do other activities that would not give room for rest and spiritual reflection. This day could be for church services, good family and friendship cherished moments, or in activities that bring joy and relaxation. This is one of the most difficult habits to put into practice. Having a time of Sabbath will not happen without planning and preparation. If you can't find a whole day to rest, begin with a morning or afternoon and work on it from there. Once this habit is in your life, you won't know how you got through your week without it.

#5 Find a Spiritual Mentor

Mature believers in our lives provide us with guidance, insight, and practical advice in living as a Christian. Individuals we would see as a mentor have been on the path of faith for a longer period than we have. Their wisdom, knowledge, and understanding of the scriptures and working through the seasons of life become invaluable to us. Such wisdom can help you go through life having someone with whom to talk with along the way. Not only do spiritual mentors give us guidance but the model for us what living a life that is both faithful and Christ-centered truly means. They encourage and support our growth in our relationship with God and help us go deeper into the understanding of His Word.

The Big Idea

A spiritual mentor is an important person in our growth in the faith because they have journeyed longer in faith and have wisdom and knowledge that help us greatly. They will impart guidance, insight, and some practical advice on how to wade through life's challenges while exercising wisdom to make sound decisions and avoid pitfalls. Overall, this is an important consideration as you think about the need for a spiritual mentor in your life.

The Word

1 Thessalonians 5:11 *Therefore encourage one another and build one another up, just as you are doing.*

This verse brings out an important aspect of Christianity: that of mutual encouragement and support. It reminds us that, being members of Christ, we have an obligation to uplift each other's faith—whether by word, deed, or even a listening ear. In so doing, we create an atmosphere of love, support, and growth in our Christian Walk.

Putting It Into Practice

There are several ways you can find a spiritual mentor for your life. Think about someone you look up to spiritually. They may be a person who is a season ahead of you in their faith. To begin thinking about who to ask to be a mentor to you, ask to meet with a trusted person when you have a huge decision to make in your life. You may be going through a career transition or to resolve a family situation. Mentors bring experience of years and a more mature understanding of the will of God to the table. This allows them to provide biblical perspective, prayer, and practical advice that will be tailored to your strengths, interests, and spiritual gifts. Having mentor like this empowers you to start making decisions and grow in your faith.

#6 Forgiveness Focused

Forgiveness-focused is the way to our spiritual growth. We will not be able to move forward without it; we will stay stuck. Grievances, events, or even unjust treatment held onto will forever hold us back in our relationship with Jesus. Letting go of the past and looking toward the future is an open invitation for inner healing to take place in our lives. For some of us, this may have to start with forgiving ourselves. While we may be able to forgive others, it is a little difficult to forget as the mind may hold certain memories of the mistakes committed in the past. These continue to haunt us by holding us in the present and from moving into the future. It is only by forgiving that we are truly set free.

The Big Idea

Forgiveness is the key to spiritual growth and inner healing. It indicates that we have let go of his past and moved into a new future. We will therefore be free from pain of the past and begin to heal our wounds. Forgiveness helps to move us into this new season of restoration. We can then begin to restore those relationships that, because of unforgiveness, have been torn apart.

The Word

Mark 11:25 *And whenever you stand praying, forgive, if you have anything against anyone, so that your Father also who is in heaven may forgive you your trespasses.*

This passage brings out the issue of forgiveness in your life. The words of Jesus teach us to forgive whosoever wrongs us, despite the offense. The scripture is teaching us that forgiveness is not optional, but a necessary component of our faith. It is a reminder that we are to bear no grudge or resentment but give grace and forgiveness toward others as has been given to us through Christ.

Putting It Into Practice

Forgiveness in the everyday life of the Christian can be

exercised through deliberate acts of letting go of past hurts and grievances. If someone did something to hurt you, take some time to consider and pray over it. Ask God to give you grace so you can forgive whoever your offender is and release your anger or bitterness. Write a letter to the person you need to forgive; don't ever mail it. Cultivate this virtue of self-forgiveness. Begin to understand and learn that spiritual growth, restoration, and healing only take place as you learn how to forgive yourself and others. If we constantly practice forgiveness, then we begin to have a spirit characterized by grace, love, and spiritual growth.

"

Spiritual growth is not a journey of perfection, but a journey of intention. -Rick Warren

"

#7 Practicing Humility

Practicing humility is necessary if you want to emulate Jesus Christ. Jesus humbled himself throughout the course of His ministry, reflecting the important place humility held in His actions. Humility teaches us to treat everybody with respect and dignity and love; it teaches us to consider everybody else's needs above our own. Such is the mindset that will allow us to be open to the Lord's teaching and leading through His word. As we humble ourselves, our lives are conformed to the likeness of Christ as a continual reminder that everything is based on Him alone.

The Big Idea

Humility in our lives as Christians is an attitude we want to practice every day. It helps us respect, love, and dignify others; to place their needs over and above ours; and aligns us with the very character of Christ, reminding us of our dependency on God.

The Word

Luke 14:11 *For all those who exalt themselves will be humbled, and those who humble themselves will be exalted.*

The scripture teaches that the Kingdom of God is based on the virtue of humility. If we decide to humble ourselves before God by recognizing Him for what He is and by valuing others, then God will, at due time, exalt us. That is to say, greatness is seen in humility, not in recognition or self-exaltation.

Putting It Into Practice

Let's begin to flesh out what humility might look like in everyday life. We create opportunities to serve others, either through tangible acts of service or simply being present to the people in our lives. We purposefully look for ways to serve others. We might volunteer on a regular basis at a local homeless shelter, showing love and dignity to those who have been marginalized. In the humble serving of others, we not only fulfill Jesus' command to 'love our neighbors' but develop a mindset that continually reminds us of our dependence upon God. As we reflect the character of Christ, we grow in humility.

#8 Prioritize Sharing Christ

The last words of Jesus in Matthew 28 are powerful directives to us. We as the body of Christ, the church, makes sharing Christ a central focus in our lives. By sharing the message of Jesus in our life, we become every day ambassadors. We want to be able to communicate our faith effectively in everyday situations. Sharing how Jesus has touched our lives is one way we can comfort, encourage, and support others facing challenges in life. Such testimonies mean so much when someone is bereaved or perhaps going through health challenges. We want to share the great things God has done in our own lives, so we can be present and comfort others in their struggle or season of life.

The Big Idea

The bottom line is to let sharing Christ be an ordinary part of our lives. Our mouths, our hands, and feet are to share His love through kinds acts and words of encouragement and hope. Our desire to bring comfort to others as a witness of God's transformation as people face various challenges in their life.

The Word

John 3:16 *For God so loved the world that he gave his one and only Son, that whoever believes in him shall not perish but have eternal life.*

John 3:16 highlights God's amazing love towards us. God expresses His love toward us as He gave His only begotten Son, Jesus Christ, as a sacrifice for our sins and gave us eternal life as we believe in Him. This verse brings out the heart of God. It shows God's desire for us to have a personal relationship with Him. It teaches us that everybody, irrespective of his or her background or past mistakes, is able to attain salvation through this gift of salvation through the acceptance of Jesus as Savior and Lord.

Putting It Into Practice

We can share our testimonies or personal experiences about Christ and how He has changed our life. To help us share our story, write out your story. Allow the Holy Spirit to guide and direct you what to share. As we begin to share what Christ has done for us, we encourage and help others to understand the meaning of John 3:16. When we are ready to share our story, we can maximize the opportunities the Lord brings our way to share the hope and love of Jesus Christ. This will be answering the call to share Christ practically in our daily lives.

#9 Reading Scripture

Reading the Bible is paramount to Christians because it provides divine guidance, influences one's knowledge of God, lays a moral framework, brings about personal transformation, helps understand God's will, strengthens faith, and enables an individual to get attached to Him. Christians can make reading the Bible a daily habit by deciding at what time to start and with which reading plan to begin.

The Scripture is the fountain of Christian doctrine and hosts teachings that mold moral and ethical living. As 2 Timothy 3:16-17 says, "All Scripture is God-breathed and is useful for teaching, rebuking, correcting, and training in righteousness, so that the servant of God may be thoroughly equipped for every good work." Therefore, when a Christian immerses himself in the Word of God, he can grow spiritually to serve humanity effectively in answering his kingdom calling.

The Big Idea

Reading scripture spiritualizes, helps one appropriately understand God's nature, and gives one a basis for proper ethical standards. Scripture also develops an individual, is instrumental in the discernment of and dedication to God's will, and strengthens faith. It also brings about social cohesion and supports purposeful living. It is limited by giving a historical background, adds richness to worship, and eventually allows the believer to face the challenges of life armed with wisdom and confidence.

The Word

Psalm 119:105 *Your word is a lamp for my feet, a light on my path.*

This scripture illustrates the changing power of God's Word. He has become my Lamp unto my feet and Light unto my paths. The scripture not only lightens our way but guides us in life, just like a lamp, showing every step that one must take towards living intentionally and purposefully.

Putting It Into Practice

Start your daily reading of the Bible by designating a

specific time of the day, like during breakfast or before bed, and setting that time solely for the reading of the scriptures. If you want some added structure and guidance, then you can freely create a reading plan or even use apps related to reading the Bible. Keeping a journal adds depth by reflection in terms of insight and even prayers. Memorizing key verses and incorporating audio Bibles into daily routines are rich additions to engage with the scriptures. Find an accountability partner or group for mutual support and encouragement in this journey of discipleship.

#10 Spiritual Retreat

Participating in spiritual retreats is great tool to living an intentional Christian life. Your relationship with God is taken to a deeper level with a focus on prayer, meditation, studying scripture, and being able to hear God's voice when there aren't so many distractions. Spending this time with God will grow your relationship with Him as you set apart this time for spiritual growth. The retreat refreshes you, offering rest from life's demands. Most settings guide you to review your life, realign priorities and reconnect with your faith and core values. Engaging in a longer retreat experience may be a possibility to help you grow in faith and character. The community and fellowship with other believers grow us spiritually. As you practice various ways to retreat, they usually include a quiet location, setting apart dedicated time, disconnecting from technology, meditation, scripture study, silence practice, worship, journaling, connecting with nature, and seeking spiritual guidance.

The Big Idea,

Taking time for a spiritual retreat helps us to gain clarity, renew the spirit, seek guidance, and live more intentionally. You create a sacred space when you are away from the many distractions you face. Blocking a period of time away will help you to not only grow closer to God but also build community with other retreat goers.

The Word

Psalm 46:10 *Be still, and know that I am God; I will be exalted among the nations, I will be exalted in the earth.*

It is the direct invitation from God for us to be still and know that He is in control and near. It is a call to pause from our normal tasks and be quiet. The command to be still itself speaks of ceasing to strive and allowing God to work according to His power and purpose. By spending time for reflection and retreat, we are able to be still before God, letting Him speak, guide, and reveal Himself to us. In the stillness with God, we are drawn to press on and draw nearer to God, finding rest and clarity about our faith on this journey.

Putting It Into Practice

Find ways to have a spiritual retreat. If you can't begin with a whole weekend, start with an afternoon. You will want to find a quiet place, time alone, and off-grid from technology. With these considerations, you can focus on prayer and meditation, Bible and devotional study, silence and solitude, being in nature, and spiritual consultation with other Christians or a spiritual director. By taking time away on retreat, you will have the opportunity to deepen your faith and see what God has in store for your life.

"

Investing in spiritual growth is the best investment you can make for your soul. -John Maxwell

"

#11 Investing in Spiritual Growth

As a disciple of Jesus Christ, you must make capital investments in order to grow spiritually. Taking time and energy to deepen your relationship with God, is part of the process of transformation into the image of Christ, and equips us for service. Your faith will be built up to testify to others. We can't give from an empty spiritual cup. Spiritual growth will deepen your relationship with him, transforming your character to be more and more like Christ, in order to serve more effectively. Intentionality involves the investment of time, energy, and focus on the practices that help us to grow spiritually; these disciplines include scripture reading, prayer, and listening to what the Lord has to say to us.

The Big Idea

The time spent, effort, and money invested in spiritual growth will pay off. Our desire is to grow and be close to God as we practice the spiritual disciplines. When you invest in your own personal spiritual growth, you will begin to live your life in accordance with what God desires for us. You will be enabled to become like Christ, serve others selflessly, stand up for the challenges in the world, and lead a life full of purpose through the power of the Holy Spirit.

The Word

Matthew 25:21 *His master replied, 'Well done, good and faithful servant! You have been faithful with a few things; I will put you in charge of many things. Come and share your master's happiness.'*

This verse challenges us to invest in our own spiritual development and be good stewards of what God has given us. This passage teaches that the faithful and diligent manager of resources and opportunities of God results in reward and joy in His presence. It helps underline that what we need to do is use our talents in the small things, and, in using, we may make a larger difference in the world.

Put It Into Practice

The discipline to invest in learning and spiritual growth will without a doubt make a huge difference in your life. Begin by simply blocking out time for you to engage in a time of scripture reading and prayer. Find the time of day that would work best for you. For some, it will be at the beginning of the day; for others it will be at the end of the day. You will want to find what works best for you in order to be consistent in taking time to invest in your own spiritual growth.

#12 Investing in Others

For the Christian, living intentionally means making an

investment in the lives of others. We have the opportunity to express love and compassion as we acknowledge and reconfirm the worth and value of every person. We invest in others by discipling individuals who grow spiritually and begin to flourish. We build community; we build a spiritual family. Such investments bring to life possibilities for participation and manifestation of the Gospel in the lives of others, in both word and deed. By allocating personal time and energy, you work in partnership with God in order to bring about transformation. Such a contribution lasts beyond this life into eternity. An investment in others can be something as simple as good listening, acts of kindness, mentoring, or serving.

The Big Idea

As Christians, we are called to live in community. We invest in the lives of others. We are part of God's great design to bring heaven to earth. As Christ's ambassadors, we join Him in making disciples. We participate in advancing the Kingdom by investing our life in others.

The Word

Proverbs 27:17 *As iron sharpens iron, so one person sharpens another.*

This verse brings out the idea of developing of healthy relationships and how they have the potential to positively affect our life. People can sharpen iron, just as interaction with others can help in sharpening us towards growing and maturing in our faith. By investing in the lives of other believers, we create space and the opportunity for mutual growth and edification.

Putting It Into Practice

One way that we can invest in the lives of others is through consistent involvement in a small group or church community. Engaging with one another, sharing experiences, and support are imperative in creating an environment for growth, accountability, and encouragement. This can be done by attending the small group meetings, contributing to the discussions, and intentionally trying to develop connections within the community. During the process, we can invest in others and be invested in ourselves through spiritual transformation to experience Christian community.

#13 Practicing Silence

In a world full of chaos, distractions, and noise, practicing silence and solitude is an often-forgotten aspect for discipleship. It allows us to actually have communion with God and foster a deeper relationship through prayer and reflection. It gives us bandwidth and margin for self-reflection and examination to help you align your life with your faith. Silence and solitude help you in the discernment and decision-making process, providing clarity and guidance when faced with challenges. It is important to start small and adapt solitude to your daily routines and rhythms. Ultimately, the intentional practice of silence and solitude can lead to spiritual growth and deepen your relationship with God.

The Big Idea

Being silent takes away all that distracts us and helps us to listen to what God is trying to tell us. We need this quiet time in order to develop our relationship with God. It's taking a pause and finding a place away from the world's noises for prayers, reflections, and discernment. You can only start hearing God in your life by forging out time for silence and solitude.

The Word

Psalm 46:10 *Be still, and know that I am God; I will be exalted among the nations, I will be exalted in the earth.*

This passage reminds us to be still and to know God for who He really is: a God present, powerful, and in control. In the helter-skelter of this world's busyness, stopping to be silent and alone allows the quieting of the mind and heart. When we lay down our need to control and striving for what we want, we can then find peace and trust in God's sovereignty. Through quietness, we get a better understanding of God's nature and can hear Him in our life.

Putting It Into Practice

A simple way to get started in integrating silence and solitude into your life could be to set apart a specific time each day where you shut down the distractions and deliberately spend time in quiet reflection. It could be choosing either morning or evening quiet time as a decided period for prayer, meditation, scripture reading, and personal reflection. Keeping this time consistently will help establish a daily rhythm of silence and solitude that will provide space for deepening with God and growing spiritually. Keep a journal to help you capture what God is teaching you in your time of silence with Him.

"

Time is not refundable; Use it with intention. - Madi Parkinson

"

#14 Embracing Simplicity

For most of us, embracing simplicity may mean focusing our concentration towards God and not on accumulating things. Desiring contentment for what we have, not only helps us to be grateful for our blessings, but better stewards. Whether you are cleaning up your living space, tidying up your calendar, or unplugging from technology, it is eventually going to clear out a way to have some margin in your life and fewer distractions. It will help you get your attention focused on what's most important and not worry about everything else that clutters up your life. The fewer things you have to think about, the clearer you're going to see where you want to channel your time, energy, and resources. Begin small but make progress in stages toward the things that bring serenity, fulfillment, and an intimate relationship with God. It's this kind of simplicity that helps us to actually live free, full, and meaningful lives.

The Big Idea

Embracing simplicity as a Christian will help us grow in your relationship with God and detach your life only pursuing what the world deems as important. Simplicity helps us to avoid the many distractions and temptations that come from the material world, grow gratitude, and foster contentment in our lives. We can also be better stewards of what God has entrusted to us.

The Word

1 Corinthians 7:30-31 (The Message version) *I want you to live as free of complications as possible. When you're unmarried, you're free to concentrate on simply pleasing the Master. Marriage involves you in all the nuts and bolts of domestic life and in wanting to please your spouse, leading to so many more demands on your attention. The time and energy that married people spend on caring for and nurturing each other, the unmarried can spend in becoming whole and holy instruments of God.*

This passage shows that Paul urges people to live a simple life, looking only to please God. He focused on the advantages of not being married, stating that a person is able to serve the Lord without distraction. The important revelation in these verses is that we live as unencumbered by the details of life as possible—we live simply. This passage is teaching us the value of simplicity in our lives as Christians and freedom found in focusing on our relationship with God.

Putting It Into Practice

One of the most helpful things to do to begin a simpler life is to take an inventory of basic systems you use every day. Each week, skim over your calendar to move forward only the more important ones taking out the events and tasks that don't contribute to your overall calling for your life. Begin decluttering your house by cleaning one drawer or maybe one closet. Simplify your daily routine with the most powerful habits to change your life. It means minimizing the various distractions from the most central values that exist in your life.

#15 Practice Praise

Praise allows us to show gratitude and adoration to God: even in situations where it feels impossible to show it, God is worthy of our praise. Praise demonstrates that He is sovereign and faithful regardless of our present circumstances. Through praising, our focus gets off our own life and situation and refocused on God. In the middle of whatever is going on in our life, we acknowledge His power, sovereignty, and His good plans over our lives. Besides, praising God also builds our relationship with Him. Praise draws us closer to His feet and heart in order to be aligned with His will. Another benefit is that praise makes us happy because when we praise God, our joy grows as well. As we praise, happiness meter grows as well!

The Big Idea

For us, praise is necessary to be thankful, recognize God's sovereignty over all, and to enhance our love for Him. We turn from ourselves to God through praise, placing joy and peace as we give ourselves to Him regardless of our situation. Praise empowers us to keep our hearts aligned with His purposes and to glorify His name in all aspects of our daily lives.

The Word

Psalm 63:1-4 *O God, you are my God; earnestly I seek you; my soul thirsts for you; my flesh faints for you, as in a dry and weary land where there is no water. So I have looked upon you in the sanctuary, beholding your power and glory. Because your steadfast love is better than life, my lips will praise you. So I will bless you as long as I live; in your name I will lift up my hands.*

These verses are the sigh of the deepest longing and thirst of the psalmist for God. Our souls are to thirst after God as we would physically thirst in a dry land. He beholds God's power and glory in His steadfast love and involuntarily erupts into praise and worship. Today's passage calls us into first pursuit toward God, in acknowledgment that He alone is worthy of adoration and praise—not only on Sundays but every day of the week.

Putting It Into Practice

Starting your day with praise will open your day to the presence of the Holy Spirit. Find your favorite hymn or worship song and play it as you get ready for the day. Play a tune while you are getting dressed, during your commute, or even while you are working throughout your day. This daily worship invites the presence of the Lord into your day.

"

The seeds you plant in your spiritual garden will determine the fruit you bear in life. -Joyce Meyer

"

#16 Engaging in the Arts

Throughout history, we can see Christian influence in the art world. Art can be an inspiration and uplift our spirits in ways no other medium of expression seems able to do. Through this art, one can grow in understanding themselves, their faith, and the world in which we live. Whether it be music, visual arts, literature, or even dance, the arts remind us of God's transcendence and how it relates us to something bigger than ourselves. Through the arts, we are allowed to see the beauty and detailed of creation by God. Engaging in the arts could also be a way of worshiping and be a means to glorify God. We are not worshiping the art, but rather to using it as a tool to connect us to God. Art can be an effective means and witness of the Good News. Art engages our emotions and allows us to experience what the artist intended.

The Big Idea

Art helps us to be inspired, encouraged, and draws us in to see the deeper things of who we are, our faith, and the world around us. By creating art as an act of worship, we can offer our talents in a way to glorify God through them, share our beliefs with others, and deepen our relationship with Him.

The Word

Exodus 35:31-33 *And he has filled him with the Spirit of God, with wisdom, with understanding, with knowledge and with all kinds of skills—to make artistic designs for work in gold, silver and bronze, to cut and set stones, to work in wood and to engage in all kinds of artistic crafts.*

This scripture brings up the area of God's gifting, equipping artists with particular talents for their mandate to produce works that inspire and have meaning. It emphasizes the need to use such talents for the honor and praise of God, to instruct others, and in creative expressions that reflect the beauty and creativity of God.

Putting It Into Practice

Take some time to think about how you might incorporate art into your life in order to focus on all that is beautiful, good, and true. You could do some painting, play an instrument, write songs, or create other pieces of art that allow you to worship, reflect, and give your faith meaning. Making space for creativity within daily routines allows us to grow deeper in our relationship with God. Art can also be a tool to share your faith with others. Before we had the printing press, artists depicted the biblical story through stained glass. Discover those hidden gems in a sanctuary near you.

#17 Explore Forms of Prayer

Different forms of prayer will draw you closer to God. Too often we have our laundry list of what we are asking God for in our life. As we explore various styles of prayer, you will be able to experience God in new and different ways. Here are some methods that you may want to explore: meditation, contemplation, intercessory prayers, or journaling. The various approaches of prayer enable us to order to communicate with God. Taking different approaches to prayer might help you learn other different types of prayers that get out of your routine or rut and allow you to grow spiritually.

The Big Idea

Trying out different forms and practices of prayer will help you find a method which works for you in a particular season of your life. Utilizing prayers from the scriptures, Christians throughout history, and liturgies open your spirit to various forms of prayer that may not be familiar to you.

The Word

Romans 8:26 *Likewise the Spirit helps us in our weakness. For we do not know what to pray for as we ought, but the Spirit himself intercedes for us with groanings too deep for words.*

Sometimes we don't even know how to prayer. This verse encourages us that if we don't know what to pray or how to pray, the Holy Spirit will intercede for us and helps us in our weaknesses. This passage teaches reliance on the leading and help of the Spirit in our life of prayer, with assurance that He will help us to speak, even when we do not know how.

Putting It Into Practice

Begin with a regular, scheduled time each day for prayer and reflection. Start with traditional prayer, then progress to meditation on a Psalm or writing out your prayers by journaling as a means of being more personal with God. Find or go to workshops or retreats on prayer where you learn and practice these different forms of prayer together with other Christians; this provides support and a strong environment to enrich your spiritual growth. This kind of diversification in prayers will help deepen one's relationship with God and increase one's spiritual quotient.

"

Intentional spiritual growth is a conscious choice to evolve into the best version of yourself. -Beth Moore

"

#18 Spiritual Formation

Spiritual formation is the process of being formed into the image of Christ. Participation in spiritual practices—prayer, meditation, and study of scriptures—will begin to form you into His likeness. This process of intentional spiritual formation will guide you to grow in your faith, allow your character be built, and understand the word and ways of Jesus. The spiritual disciplines are tools to help you in that process of being conformed to the image of Christ. A spiritual director could give guidance in this journey of reflection and spiritual growth.

The Big Idea

Spiritual formation helps you develop a personal, close relationship with God, increase your faith, and to align your life with God. Through the spiritual disciplines, we are guided towards knowing not only ourselves but the Lord in a more intimate way. Spiritual formation equips us to be like Jesus and to withstand the challenges of life in a hopeful, assured manner, leading a life that is firmly grounded in scripture, based on truth, and filled with grace.

The Word

2 Corinthians 3:18 *And we all, who with unveiled faces contemplate the Lord's glory, are being transformed into his image with ever-increasing glory, which comes from the Lord, who is the Spirit.*

This passage illustrates the change that came from beholding the glory of the Lord. As we spend time in the presence of God, study His Word, and fellowship with Him in prayer, we are gradually molded into His image. The very process of spiritual formation is an ever-increasing likeness to that of Jesus Christ, guided and empowered by the Holy Spirit through faith.

Putting It Into Practice

This idea of spiritual formation can be realized in one very practical way: Find somebody who can be a director of spiritual formation in your reflections and growth. The director of spiritual formation is a trained person who offers support, guidance, and motivation to deepen your relationship with God and to discern His will for your life. Spiritual directors can help you explore your spiritual practices, reflect on your experiences, and identify where things might need to shift and change. Spiritual direction provides individual guidance and support in finding ways to live a purposeful life following Jesus.

#19 Christian Meditation

What makes Christian meditation different from the rest is that other types of meditation empty your mind. For Jesus followers, meditation is based on the scripture. Exploring

Christian meditation can help benefit believers in living intentionally for several reasons. Through meditation, we cultivate stillness and listening to God in silence and contemplative prayer. We can experience an increased awareness of God's presence and guidance by stopping and being quiet before the Lord. Through this spiritual practice we can overcome distractions and temptations, understand deep reflections of scriptures, realize our self-awareness, and spend time in reflection of your thoughts and actions.

The Big Idea

Discovering Christian meditation can more fully open your life to the Holy Spirit's working in and through you. Biblical mediation will often guide you to dive deeper into scripture to guide your heart, mind, and body towards Christlikeness. It brings us into the presence of God, focused on gratitude of what God has done and is doing in our life.

The Word

Joshua 1:8 *Keep this Book of the Law always on your lips; meditate on it day and night, so that you may be careful to do everything written in it. Then you will be prosperous and successful.*

This scripture emphasizes the importance of meditating on God's Word, day and night, allowing it to guide your thoughts and actions. By immersing yourself in Scripture regularly, you can align yourself with God's will and experience abundance in your life.

Putting It Into Practice

Position yourself to be in a place where you are able to sit in silence and reflect on a passage of scripture. Begin with just five or ten minutes. Find a comfortable place to sit or kneel where there will be few distractions. Let your thoughts center on the words of God. Allow the Holy Spirit to guide your thoughts and feelings as you meditate on the passage. Let the words go right into the heart of your soul, and, in so doing, open yourself to receive whatever insight or guidance He may intend to bring to you. Meditate on that verse throughout the day and begin to turn your thoughts toward God. This can create peace and clarity in the soul and allow a deeper relationship with Him.

#20 Hospitality

Hospitality is a practice that is encouraged over and over again in the scriptures. We are to share with others in need and practice generosity whether in our home or wherever we are. As we show God's love through welcoming every person, despite their background, we can be imitators of Christ's character and show kindness to strangers. Hospitality fosters a sense of community in the body of believers in the church and through that activity, we build unity and fellowship. Christians can demonstrate their love for their neighbors by lavish generosity in the sharing resources and modeling God's provision. Hospitality offers Christians an opportunity to engage in evangelism and discipleship: to share the Good News and to build meaningful relationships. In practice, hospitality becomes an intentional attempt to live out your faith in everyday situations.

The Big Idea

Hospitality is important to live out our faith because it is part of the Biblical teaching. Through hospitality, we reflect the love of Christ, build community, and demonstrate God's generosity. It facilitates evangelism and discipleship in everyday, ordinary ways.

The Word

1 Peter 4:8 *Above all, love each other deeply, because love covers over a multitude of sins.*

This verse in 1 Peter underlines love's role in relationships. It is through this deep love that the flaws and shortcomings of the person can be overlooked, just as the love of God overshadows our sins. Practicing hospitality is a concrete expression of such deep love to others by providing an atmosphere of welcome and acceptance where relationships can blossom.

Putting It Into Practice

Intentional hospitality can be effectively incorporated into everyday life by opening up the home and heart to others. Invite friends over, your neighbors, and fellow believers in the church for a meal or a time of fellowship. One of my favorite ways is gathering others around the fire pit. Our desire is to create a space for others, letting them feel welcomed and valued. Think about an event you can create to invite others to share in conversation and fellowship. You can even include food to enhance the experience.

"

The path of intentional spiritual growth is paved with self-awareness, self-love, and self-compassion. - T.D. Jakes

"

Physical Capital

The investment in physical capital as a Christian involves good care of the body as the temple of the Holy Spirit. In this focus, we are working towards good health, self-care, and physical fitness. By being healthy, we are preparing ourselves to serve with joy and enthusiasm. This section shows that God's greater purpose can be achieved in our lives by living a healthy lifestyle of proper diet, exercise, and rest. We are not able to serve, if our health is failing. Once health is repositioned to be a stewardship matter, our desire is to care for what God has entrusted to us in this life. Just as we invest in spiritual growth and relationships, so, too, taking care of our body is an integral part of our responsibility as Christians. Through a disciplined lifestyle, habits, and intentional self-care practices, we can create a pattern of living that reflects our commitment to honor God through our body. As we include our physical capital into our stewardship of life, the goal is to begin making choices that lead us to honor God through our bodies.

#21 Stewarding Resources

A primary component of our life as a Christian is to be a faithful steward of everything that has been entrusted to us. This implies that we are cautious and grateful in managing our time, our talents, and our relationships. Being good stewards of what He has given us, we honor God and live as caretakers in His creation. This attitude enables us to live a gracious and humble life, realizing all we possess belongs ultimately to God and has been given to us for some special purpose. Stewardship is at the center of living out our faith in concrete and practical ways.

Being good stewards, demonstrates that we are able to show our faithfulness and gratitude for what has been entrusted to us. The essence of stewardship can be seen as a reflection of our faith. It calls into play the values that are central to the teachings of Jesus: generosity, responsibility, and compassion.

The Big Idea

Purposeful living in Christ means being good stewards of all of our resources. Handling material things, time, talents, and relationships in a way that glorifies God expresses appreciation for all the things that He did and gave to us. We exercise stewardship over God's creation as we prove to be good stewards with what He has given us. Our faithfulness in small things gives way for Him to entrust us with even more for our life.

The Word

Genesis 1:28 *God blessed them and said to them, 'Be fruitful and increase in number; fill the earth and subdue it.*

Rule over the fish in the sea and the birds in the sky and over every living creature that moves on the ground.'

The verse reminds that God give His people the responsibility of stewardship to care for and rule over creation. This involves the exercising of good management in the use of resources and being a faithful steward to the earth. Christians are called to responsibly take up dominion with love, compassion, and respect accorded to God's creation.

Putting It Into Practice

As you being to view your life as a faithful steward, begin by taking an inventory on what resources you have and how you are using them. Consider ways that you can better manage your time, talents, relationships, and material things in ways that bring God more glory and serve others. As you look at everything you own, you may want to consider downsizing or simplifying your life. Think about your calendar. Is how you spend your time seen as being a wise use what the Lord has given to you? By examining your life, begin to think about how you can be more purposeful in decisions that flesh out stewardship and generosity in your life.

#22 Body Life

This teaching concerning our bodies as living sacrifices is deeply rooted in biblical teachings and principles. It is articulated in Paul's letter, where he encourages believers to present their bodies as a living sacrifice, holy and pleasing to God. This is a symbolic way of showing spiritual devotion, gratitude, and worship toward God. By recognizing our bodies as temples of the Holy Spirit, we will value ourselves and care for our bodies as an expression of gratitude toward the gift of life. Tending to our bodies aligns with the biblical principle of stewardship, enabling us to serve God and other people more effectively. The deliberate decisions that we make should be a witness to everyone around us of God's power in our lives, offering opportunities to share the Good News of faith. The exercise of discernment and self-control in how we treat our bodies can create an intentional lifestyle which brings glory to God.

The Big Idea

Christians are to treat and care for their bodies as an offering to God that signifies spiritual commitment and respect. The message brought by Paul to the Romans emphasizes the idea of presenting our bodies as a living sacrifice, holy and pleasing to God. By regarding our body as the temple of the Holy Spirit, we can honor life and practice faithful stewardship.

The Word

1 Corinthians 6:19-20 *Do you not know that your bodies are temples of the Holy Spirit, who is in you, whom you have received from God? You are not your own; you were bought at a price. Therefore, honor God with your bodies.*

This verse reminds us how our bodies are sacred and worthy temples of the Holy Spirit. We are to glorify God in our bodies by taking care of them, being reverent, remembering that we do not belong to ourselves, as we have been purchased for a price—the sacrifice of our Lord Jesus Christ.

Putting It Into Practice

This very concept of treating our bodies as a living sacrifice would play out in everyday life through prioritizing self-care practices that include regular exercise, healthy eating, and adequate rest. Intentional concern for the care of our physical well-being indeed honors God. We are responsible for our bodies. Begin to look at how you care for your own body. Look at your daily habits and routines that specifically focus on your body. Think of one goal you would like to work on to better care for your body.

"

The greatest wealth is health. –Virgil

"

#23 Personal Cleanliness

Personal hygiene is important to the Christian way of living on several levels. Hygiene is a way to steward your body by recognizing that it is a temple of the Holy Spirit. This demonstrates respect for life as a gift from God. Personal cleanliness contributes towards the way of loving others, avoiding the transmission of diseases which promotes good health. As Christians personal hygiene practices should aim to steward our bodies well. This gives glory to God. In emphasizing these practices, we know we are doing our part in caring for what the Lord has entrusted to us.

The Big Idea

Personal hygiene is important for a Christian in order to live purposefully in daily life. As we keep our body clean as the temple of the Holy Spirit, we are also taking care of others from unnecessary illness. Good personal hygiene stems from biblical principles and leads to a life of stewardship, wisdom, and spiritual discipline—the outflow of a faithful life.

The Word

2 Corinthians 7:1 *Therefore, since we have these promises, dear friends, let us purify ourselves from everything that contaminates body and spirit, perfecting holiness out of reverence for God.*

This verse highlights the need for cleansing ourselves in a physical and spiritual way out of reverence for God. We are called to live a life of personal cleanliness as Christians to glorify God and reflect His holiness in our lives.

Putting It Into Practice

We can't do everything at once, but choose one area of care for your body that you might focus on to begin cleaning up. It may be a daily habit of showering or being more intentional about washing your hands in order to prevent disease. The development of daily routines may include brushing teeth, grooming nails, or managing your hair. Which do you want to work on first? How often do you want to implement this practice? Start small and build on the habits that help care for your body in the area of personal hygiene.

#24 Healthy Diet

There are several reasons we are to focus on healthy eating. Not only is it a way to be a good steward over our bodies, but we are able to serve God even better if we are physically fit. When we exercise restraint and self-discipline, we are able to avoid the foods that are not as healthy for our bodies. A healthy diet works in conjunction with spiritual growth. When we focus on health, we can more effectively manage all of the other areas of our life. When we are disciplined in one area of our life, it typically spills out to other segments as well. As we nourish our bodies with foods that we need, we fuel ourselves in order to live out God's purpose for our life more readily each day.

The Big Idea

A healthy, balanced diet will give us self-discipline and a way to make wise choices to steward our bodies well. As we focus on eating a healthy diet, we will make an intentional investment in the body God has entrusted to us.

The Word

1 Corinthians 10:31 *So, whether you eat or drink, or whatever you do, do all to the glory of God.*

These words of scripture remind us that everything we do, even down to the food we eat, should be done in a manner that glorifies God. A good diet will honor God by taking care of our bodies, which are given by Him. Our eating habits can show our commitment to live according to His will and will bring glory to God.

Putting It Into Practice

Think about what you eat in a normal day. Gradually increase your intake of fruits, vegetables, whole grains, and lean proteins if needed to begin taking better care of your physique. It may mean to add more unprocessed foods. It may be to limit sugary drinks and processed snacks. Take some intentional time each week to plan and prepare healthy meals and snacks for the days ahead. Meal prepping is a great way to prepare for the means during the week when things can become very hectic. Start small and build to develop those healthy eating habits to care for your body. Remember, progress, not perfection.

#25 Body Image

Body image is extremely relevant to Christian life because it can impact your self-esteem, worthiness, and perception of God's creation which is YOU! As believers we understand and know that we are fearfully and wonderfully made in the image of God. We are to care for our body as His temple, a place that houses the Holy Spirit. After all, we are a gift from God. We are to be treasured, cared for, and respected. Looking not only at our appearance, we also look at our inner beauty and the attributes valued by God. We hold fast to a body image that is positive and deeply rooted in our faith.

The Big Idea

Body image is such an important concept in a person's life. It affects our self-esteem, self-worth, and views of God's handiwork formed in you. As we begin to embrace a positive body image, we are grateful for the beautiful work of God's creation in us.

The Word

Psalm 139:14 *I praise you because I am fearfully and wonderfully made; your works are wonderful, I know that full well.*

This very scripture reminds us that we are fearfully and wonderfully made in God's image. We praise God for the construction of our bodies created in His image. We are to appreciate the beauty and uniqueness of our bodies. With this truth, we can fight negative self-image and find confidence in our identity as children of God.

Putting It Into Practice

Christians can live out and apply the concept of self-care of their body by seeing their body as a gift of God and a temple worthy of respect; such an attitude will result in good body care. Respect for our body and maintenance of a good body image witness faith in the creation of God. Begin by thinking of one of your physical attributes that you love. Accentuate it. Let it shine! Building on that area, you can love and appreciate others areas of your body as you see it through the eyes of the Creator.

#26 Physical Exercise

To Christians, exercise more than just the means of taking care of a person's health. It's an act of worship and stewarding your life. It's a way to honor God and respect the body that God has given to us. Through exercise, we develop the habits and discipline of self-control. Working out helps our bodies to balance our life in other areas of our life as well. This helps us in our overall well-being. In and of itself, exercise is a practical way of bringing balance into our life. As we exercise, it's important that our heart remains focused on the priorities God has given us and that we do not turn exercise into an idol.

Big Idea

Exercising regularly means glorifying God through our body as a temple of the Holy Spirit. It emboldens not just physical health but the spiritual discipline of self-control and holiness, eventually enhancing our overall well-being. Moderation in one's exercise allows it to sufficiently mirror one's faith without contradicting the greater intent of God.

The Word

1 Corinthians 6:19-20 *Do you not know that your bodies are temples of the Holy Spirit, who is in you, whom you have received from God? You are not your own; you were bought at a price. Therefore honor God with your bodies.*

This passage reminds the Corinthians that their bodies are not their own but are temples of the Holy Spirit. It is within this context that we as Christians have the opportunity to glorify God with our bodies—by taking care of them, keeping them with respect, and practicing the stewardship of the physical body that God has entrusted to us.

Putting It Into Practice

If you have not exercised lately, be sure to check with your medical provider to determine any limitations you might have. Beginning a daily or weekly routine of taking a walk or some other form or exercise will help you to start. We all have to start somewhere. Get a little braver and add a class or group that may interest you, be it Pilates, cycling, or dance. Exercising in group settings helps to keep morale high and gives a feeling of belonging and accountability.

"

Physical fitness is not only one of the most important keys to a healthy body, it is the basis of dynamic and creative intellectual activity. - John F. Kennedy

"

#27 Engaging in Hobbies

We are human beings and not 'human doings.' We want to cultivate balance and rest in life and one way is through engaging in hobbies. A time of recreation provides a break from daily routines what helps you both in body and mind. As you discover new hobbies, you will be able to broaden your interests and develop your talents. Hobbies can open the door to developing relationships with others that you may not ever meet in another context. This avenue becomes a bridge to be salt and light in the public areaa. Through leisure activities, you will be able to have balance in your life as well as an outlet for stress.

The Big Idea

Hobbies are recreational activities you do in your life that help to balance your life and use your God-given talents. It becomes a way connect with people of like minds have similar interests and build connections in the community.

Hobbies can be part of an intentional life to build relationships with neighbors and acquaintances.

The Word

James 1:17 *Every good and perfect gift is from above, coming down from the Father of the heavenly lights, who does not change like shifting shadows.*

In this passage we see that all talents and skills are given as gifts. It's important to not only recognize the gift but the giver of all good things. Remember all that we are and have is a gift from God and we are to use them to serve others and glorify Him.

Putting It Into Practice

Think of something that you have wanted to learn to do or that you have enjoyed in the past but have not engaged in recently. Brainstorm ideas: Do you like to garden? Play mahjong? Pickle ball? Review your schedule to see where you would fit it in. Think about all of the equipment you need for this particular hobby. Discover others that have the same interests. Connect with them and enjoy your recreational time!

#28 Prioritizing Mental Health

Your mental health is important and interlinks with all of the other areas of your life. It impacts your life spiritually, with your relationships, and overall wellbeing. As you make your mental health a priority, you will not only benefit from these efforts, but those around you will as well. It is a wise investment of your time, energy, and money. It's not a weakness to invest in your mental health as a Christian;

rather, it's a proactive step toward living purposefully, serving others, and enjoying full engagement with God in the abundant life He has for us. Taking action can be very empowering—to make deliberate actions toward your mental wellness can help you live out your faith to the full, serve others effectively, and ultimately open oneself up to the full life which God intended for you.

Big Idea

Your mental health is an essential element in your walk with Jesus. It not only affects your spiritual life, but also your emotional wellbeing, and relationships with others. Focusing on it will help you grow in your faith, balance your emotional life, improve your relationships, and deal with the stigma that is attached by others in the Christian community.

The Word

Psalm 34:4-5 *I sought the Lord, and he answered me; he delivered me from all my fears. Those who look to him are radiant; their faces are never covered with shame.*

This passage emphasizes the desire and need to seek the Lord when faced with fear and anxiety. It is by turning our eyes toward God and investing in our personal mental health that we are delivered from our fears and shame. Developing the ability to trust God's promises and turn toward His presence to give our lives peace and radiance frees us to live life with purpose and fullness of life.

Putting It Into Practice

Begin by prioritizing your own mental health. Too often, we neglect our own wellbeing because we fail to put up necessary boundaries. We put everyone else's needs before our own. Even on the airplane, we are told to put the oxygen mask on ourselves before others. Stop to think about how you might benefit from applying boundaries in your own life. Take action to engage in counseling or joining support groups where you can air your problems openly and find insights into them in a faith-based atmosphere of help. These practices, therefore, not only enhance your emotional and spiritual well-being but also the capacity to serve others with renewed strength and clarity.

#29 Emotional Well-being

As a Christian, investing in your emotional well-being is important because you value yourself exactly the way God created you—in His image, emotions and all. Godly regard for your emotional well-being is reflected in the scriptures, with Jesus Himself showing compassion and empathy. Looking after your emotional well-being will allow you to live according to God's original plan and to love others as you love yourself, as taught in Mark 12:31. It helps you to handle stress, stay resilient, and meet any challenge with a Christ-centered view. Emotional stewardship boosts your relationships and supports your personal growth and development. As you are able to positively handle your emotional life you are able to live more fully into your God-given purpose.

The Big Idea

It is important to take care of your emotional life, as it deals with your creation in God's image, including the fact that you are a feeling being. Understanding emotional health means you will live according to what God wants you to be and to become.

The Word

Psalm 34:18 *The Lord is close to the brokenhearted and saves those who are crushed in spirit.*

The passage reminds us that God is close to the brokenhearted and comforts them. As Christians, we may be consoled by the fact that God is concerned about our feelings, for He is always present to heal and restore our souls whenever we are plagued by various emotions whether it be stress, worry, or anxiety.

Putting It Into Practice

Begin to regularly write down your thoughts and emotions to better understand your emotional well-being. This approach will help you to begin to deal with feelings constructively and discover greater clarity on your experiences. Engage in a supportive community or small group where you can share your experiences openly. This kind of a network gives you not only emotional support but spiritual accountability to help you navigate the challenges of life more effectively and with wisdom from others.

"

Every action has an impact; choose wisely the impact you want to have. –Unknown

"

#30 Seeking Support

Having support is necessary to living in purpose as a Christian for a host of reasons. Support really does keep you in check with what is going on in your life. As you surround yourself in Christian community, you will have others to walk alongside you as you go through difficult seasons in your life. With such a community, you also receive emotional and spiritual support for the challenges you face. Community and fellowship help to facilitate commonality and you have shared purpose, community, and discipleship. Having others around you will help you learn and grow as you journey on the road together. This support will not give you guidance as you go through your situation together but it will empower you to help others going through similar situations in the future. We are blessed to be a blessing to others.

The Big Idea

One of the keys to managing a tough period in your life is having a supportive network to help you through it. The emotional and spiritual encouragement that comes through a community offers not only belonging and shared purpose for times when it feels like things are just getting too tough.

The Word

Galatians 6:2 *Bear one another's burdens, and so fulfill the law of Christ.*

This verse in Galatians strongly points out the help and support that must be given to each other within the Christian community. We must come together as the body of Christ, bearing each other's burdens. By so doing, we are faithful to love one another even as He loved us. This verse teaches us about the value of mutual support and moving on together.

Putting It Into Practice

One of the most supportive practices you can implement into your life is to engage in a small group. Small groups offer not only the opportunity for spiritual growth but to bear one another's burdens as you experience life together. There are times in your life where you may want to seek out a mentor or spiritual director. Mentors are able to offer you tailored support and accountability, which can give you clarity in a particular season of your life. As you focus on building Christian community into your life, you also have opportunity to build strong support, promote spiritual growth, and have your life focused on God's purpose for you.

#31 Dressing to Honor Your Body

Living intentionally as a Christian means your actions and choices have to be from the heart, even down to how you dress. As we dress to honor our body, we are respecting the frame we have been given. As we chose clothing that is appropriate for us, we are not only showing our outer appearance but our inner qualities as well. You can dress stylishly and show off your uniqueness while showing modesty and respect in the values that bring honor to Christ. We are careful to be modest in our choices and dress as we want to be addressed.

The Big Idea

This involves dressing in a manner that respects your body, so you can live into your kingdom calling as a Christian. As you make choices of what to wear, align your lifestyle with principles depicted in scripture. These guidelines still allow you to dress stylishly and personally while expressing your commitment to God.

The Word

1 Corinthians 6:19-20 *Do you not know that your bodies are temples of the Holy Spirit, who is in you, whom you have received from God? You are not your own; you were bought at a price. Therefore honor God with your bodies.*

The scripture reminds us that our bodies are temples of the Holy Spirit and that they belong to Him. Respect is to be given to God, even with our bodies, in terms of dress code. As we dress, we show our character. It reflects our values and principles in life. As we dress modestly and decently, we are giving respect to God by living a life that is pleasing in His sight.

Putting It Into Practice

Begin by taking an inventory of your clothes closet. Which articles of clothing give honor to your body? Which pieces don't bring out the best in you? Start to make two piles: 1. Keep and 2. Give away. Wear clothes that reflect the best characteristics of your body. By dressing this way, you are showing respect to your body and presenting it as a valued creation of God. You are also creating a positive environment of respect toward all people you meet.

#32 Rule Over Your Body

As we prioritize care for our body, we are giving honor to God as well as building up your own self-worth. How you rule over your body becomes a testimony of your faith to others. We are able to exercise self-control and discipline over what we eat, how we exercise, and how much rest we get. In taking our physical health seriously, we are able to control our urges of what we eat, drink, and put into our body. In caring for our bodies, we are able to express gratitude for what God has entrusted to us and be good stewards of the frame we have in this life.

The Big Idea

Since God gave you the gift of life, taking good care of your body shows appreciation and respect for His creation. As we make wise choices and exercise control over our body, we want to be wise and faithful stewards of the gift of life that we have been given.

The Word

1 Corinthians 6:12 *All things are lawful for me, but not all things are helpful. All things are lawful for me, but I will not be dominated by anything.*

Even though we are set free in Christ, the scripture teaches us not to be mastered by anything—be it overeating or substance abuse. We must not let our flesh control us in any area of our lives but exercise discipline and self-control.

Putting It Into Practice

Here is a challenge for you. Record how you care for your

body for a week. Write down how much rest you are getting. Make a list of what foods you are eating. Take note of what you are doing for exercise. After you have taken this inventory, develop a plan using just a couple of reflective questions. What is one thing that I can do to improve what I am consuming foodwise? How can I implement some kind of movement (walking, biking, tennis, etc.) into my day at least 2-3 times a week?

"

Your health account, your bank account, they're the same thing. The more you put in, the more you can take out. -Jack LaLanne

"

#33 Remember to Rest

Understanding the value of rest is essential as we become intentionally focused with our life. By resting regularly, you model God's pattern—stop, literally take time off—to catch up, reflect, and worship, just as He did when creation was complete. Rhythms of rest will help prevent exhaustion and burnout. By regularly resting, you are demonstrating that there is more to life than productivity. In a world that never stops and hyper focuses on busyness, the example of being an intentional rest-taker sets a counterbalance everything around us. By practicing rest in our own life, we inspire others to take another look at the priorities of life. As we deliberately rest, we acknowledge our own limitations knowing that our accomplishments are a result of God working in us and even in spite of us at times.

The Big Idea

Rest not only provides balance in our life but it's also proactive in keeping our body healthy. We are to work from rest rather than rest after we have worked ourselves to death. In a world gone mad with activity, a deliberate decision to rest is a strong example to realign our life around our values and spiritual growth.

The Word

Exodus 20:8-10 *Remember the Sabbath day, to keep it holy. Six days you shall labor and do all your work, but the seventh day is the Sabbath of the Lord your God.*

The passage reminds us of the reason to rest and provide time for worship in our lives. If we set the seventh day as a sabbath to the Lord, then we are setting apart what God did, which is resting from His work of creation. Sometimes it is necessary, as this scripture communicates, to have a rest from work to be with God and rejuvenate our spirit. Just as God rested on the seventh day from all the work that He had done and was replenished, so are we to take a break from our affairs and worship, to give honor and praise to our Maker. This Sabbath keeping practice allows us to align His restorative presence in our lives.

Putting It Into Practice

Begin by taking some intentional time to rest. Implement into the rhythm of your week. You may not be able to rest for an entire day; begin by blocking of a half day to just be. Use the time to turn your mind off from the pressures of the day, read some Scripture, pray, or sit in the quiet, letting yourself refocus on your life. You may want to set up a "technology-free" zone or period in your home. All devices—phones, TVs, and computers—are switched off during this time to minimize disturbance and create some peaceful rest. This will help you to focus much on personal conversations, reading, or doing some other relaxing activity that gives your mind and spirit rest.

#34 Your Body is a Vessel

Recognizing that your body is a vessel for holy living holds heavy significance on many levels. Our body has been given as a gift. We have been entrusted as a faithful steward to take care of this body. Your body is the temple of the Holy Spirit which calls us to a lifestyle that gives glory to God. It is because a whole-person approach in aligning body, mind, and spirit with God's will accelerates health and spiritual growth. Honoring your body is a strong witness to others around you, which will can begin conversations with others. As you take care of your body as a vessel you will be able to better accomplish God's work on Earth; you contribute towards the establishment of His Kingdom here.

The Big Idea

Understand that your body is meant for purposeful living. So, take responsibility over your health, managing it in a godly way and treating your body as a holy tabernacle of the Holy Spirit. This kind of attitude toward health will bring about not only personal and spiritual well-being but also make strong statements to others and may open opportunities to share your faith and expand God's Kingdom.

The Word

Romans 9:21 *Does not the potter have the right to make out of the same lump of clay some pottery for special purposes and some for common use?*

Romans 9:21 reinforces God's sovereignty over human destiny by relating this very imagery of a potter at work with the clay. Here, God is in a position to create people for different activities. As we care for the vessel we have been given, we acknowledge God's hand on our life to serve Him in the way He has designed us.

Putting It Into Practice

Just as a sailor cares for the ship, we are to care for our body. As you think through how you care for your vessel, how might you better prepare your physical life to more faithfully serve Him. How might you better align your body, mind, and spirit to the things of God? What area of your life needs attention? What practices or habits do you need to put in place to order your life around your life's purpose?

#35 Hydration

When you get focused on living an intentional life you look at all components of good health. Hydration is a big part of that! We can live days without food; we can't live without water. Although we typically drink a variety of beverages, our bodies are made to take in water. Water keeps the body in good working condition and helps us to function in our daily activities. This very simple step toward good health of keeping hydrated will lay the foundation for living purposefully and wholeheartedly being ready for the service or purpose to which God has called you.

The Big Idea

A living, purposeful Christian takes care of his body, mind, and spirit; proper hydration is part of that. If you drink enough water to be hydrated, you will be able to glorify the physical vessel that God gave you to do, in a more effective way, the God-given roles and responsibilities for your life. Such an act of self-love and being disciplined reflects God's love and readies you for the purposeful service He has planned.

The Word

1 Corinthians 10:31 *So whether you eat or drink or whatever you do, do it all for the glory of God.*

This is such a great verse to remind us to live in ways that give glory to God in every breath, every action, right down to cups of cold water. It does underscore the importance of glorifying God through our bodies and bringing ourselves back into balance through hydration as a means of self-care and good stewardship. In addition to what will keep our physiological well-being by drinking enough water, we are told that our bodies are the temples of the Holy Spirit.

Putting It Into Practice

One practical way to have a focus on hydration in your daily life as a Christian is to take a reusable water bottle with you wherever you go. That way, the easy access to water will make it easier to keep hydrated throughout the day for the sake of health and the purpose of serving others effectively. You can also set reminders on your phone or jot down a hydration time-table to help you achieve your water intake goals. By making your hydration a priority in the daily routine, you are actually living out your faith—taking care of the physical vessel that God has entrusted to you.

#36 Healthcare

Ensuring your body is healthy is responsible stewardship and respect for God's creation. Good health allows us to fulfill our calling. As we prioritize routine healthcare practices, we are physically able to serve our families, churches, and communities. We put into place periodical check-ups in order to intentionally care for our bodies. We care for our own bodies through established routines and by doing so are an example to others to care for their own health as well. Other benefits of maintaining routine healthcare are to support others and improving our own life for service. As vital as health care may be, you realize that true healing and wellness are gifts from God.

The Big Idea

Paying attention to your health through practicing routine healthcare rituals is a good stewardship of God's creation. By keeping your physical being healthy, you are able to serve others, and share in spreading the message of Christ. While health care may be crucial, we ultimately depend on God ultimate healing.

The Word

3 John 1:2 *Dear friend, I pray that you may enjoy good*

health and that all may go well with you, even as your soul is getting along well.

What that means in this verse is that John prays for his friend Gaius to be healthy both in body and spirit. This is a reminder that God is concerned about the health of our bodies, just as He is with our souls' health. As Christians, we must also balance our lifestyles in keeping our bodies and souls healthy, knowing that both are very important to Him.

Put It Into Practice

One of the ways this can be integrated into your practical life is by incorporating regular visits to health professionals for regular checkups and prevention. This shows that you are indeed a good steward of your body. Plan out your year looking at the medical appointments you need to make annually or more often as directed by your healthcare professional. Map out the year taking into consideration annual physicals, dental, eye, and other specialized health care needs you may have. Write it on a calendar so the year doesn't slip by without getting your healthcare needs taken care of.

"

What you get by achieving your goals is not as important as what you become by achieving your goals. -Zig Ziglar

"

#37 Proper Posture

Embracing proper posture is not just about physical health but really includes a spiritual mindset in terms of stewarding your body. How you carry your body is indicative of your attitude about your own self-worth. Since we are called to treat our body as a temple of the Holy Spirit we even walk with respect and care for that body. Good posture supports this by trying to prevent injuries and promote efficiency within the functions of the body, so that you may serve God and others more effectively and energetically. When the body is aligned and taken good care of, you are most prepared to carry out the tasks set before you to fulfill your ministry, serving readily. We walk in the confidence of knowing that we are created by God with and for a purpose.

The Big Idea

Good posture is important, not only because it addresses bodily well-being but also because it actually is a sacred temple of the Holy Spirit. Giving attention to body alignment helps prevent injuries and keeps all parts working properly for carrying out responsibilities with greater vigor.

The Word

Hebrews 4:16 *Let us then with confidence draw near to the throne of grace, that we may receive mercy and find grace to help in time of need.*

Confidence impels us to draw near to the throne of grace, knowing full well we receive mercy and find grace to help in the time of need. We get confidence by the way we conduct ourselves. This verse reminds us again of the great privilege that, as believers, we have in coming before God-not in fear or in uncertainty, but in boldness and in assurance. This is a call into pressing into God's provision through whatever circumstance comes our way, knowing that He has purposed an intervention and stands ready and willing to extend His mercy and grace in our lives. That we may go out with a more profound understanding, and confidently approach Him. We can then experience His sufficiency of love and care for whatever circumstance we may go through in life.

Putting It Into Practice

Correct posture can be applied in your daily life by first learning to be aware of body alignment while sitting, standing, and moving. While at your desk, position your chair so that your feet can rest on the floor or on a small stool, your back is supported, and the computer screen is at eye level with your head arched a little to avoid slouching. Incorporate stretches and some strengthening exercises to improve core muscles, which are important in maintaining good posture. The more you practice these adjustments, the more your body will get used to holding itself in a manner that honors and cares for its structure so that you may serve with more energy and sustainability.

#38 Managing Stress

Intentional living as a Christian means structuring your behaviors, actions, and thoughts in concert with your faith. The healthy mechanisms of dealing with life keep nurturing emotional and mental well-being, allowing you to manage stress and negative feelings and provide clarity for living more intentionally. By coping with stress in a healthy manner, you show the character of Christ in the most inconsequential acts: love, patience, and kindness. It is also witness, since it exemplifies the transformation possible because of our faith. This attention to holistic well-being is central to God's desire for comprehensive health for us all, that we might serve Him and live out our Christian calling. Minimizing stress in our life frees us to live the life we were created to live.

The Big Idea

As we align our life with scripture, we notice that Jesus never seemed to be stressed! We are to create enough margin in our life in order to minimize the amount of stress in our life. By creating more space in our life for what God has called us to do, we are better suited to live out our calling with joy and not stress.

The Word

Matthew 6:34 *Therefore do not worry about tomorrow, for tomorrow will worry about itself. Each day has enough trouble of its own.*

This scripture tells us to live in the present, leaving the future to God's plans. We are not to be preoccupied with anxieties about the future but to deal with the challenges of each new day with prayer, optimism, hope, and faith.

Putting It Into Practice

Probably the best way to control stress in life would be through regular mindfulness or Christian meditation. This means to simply sit quietly for a few minutes each day, breathing deeply, and being in the present moment. This practice would allow for a decluttering of the mind, decrease anxiety, and give you emotional strength. Other practical ways to lessen stress in your life might include doing exercises, such as daily walking or hitting the gym for workouts. Physical exercises will not just keep your body fit but can also release your stress by increasing your endorphins, naturally uplifting and improving your mood. With those things, you will be able to handle stressors easier and live a well-balanced life.

#39 Simple Lifestyle

One of the most transformative decisions that Christians can make today, in their walks with God, is living simply. As we choose to live more simply on purpose, we build more space in our lives: places where distractions dwindle and our calling becomes clearer. Implementing a sense of minimalism in your life, helps you to declutter the mental and spiritual clutter and make room to better focus on God's purpose for your life. It is as we let go of the excess that we become increasingly available for ministry, service, and deep-seated joy of living with congruence in our life. Intentional simplicity gives expression to full life in faith and to serving others more powerfully.

The Big Idea

The Christian minimalist lifestyle brings us closer to God by simplifying life from all its complexities, leaving room for what is important. This means less stuff, but more importantly, it involves clearing our minds and life to be more focused on what God has set before us. In stripping away the needless, the ability to engage in meaningful ministry and service grows, bringing us closer to the calling of the Kingdom.

The Word

Luke 12:15 *Then he said to them, 'Watch out! Be on your guard against all kinds of greed; life does not consist in an abundance of possessions.'*

Here, Jesus warns greed and materialism; true life does not lie in the accumulation of possessions. As Christians, we must shift our attention to spiritual well-being rather than to material security and more importantly nurture a close relationship with God. When the heart is guarded against greed and contentment is sought in what you already have, the pace of life dramatically slows down and we are more prepared to serve when and where He calls.

Putting It Into Practice

Simplify your life. Start prioritizing what you have and what your calendar looks like. Look at your list. If it contributes to life or the spiritual purpose of your life, keep it. If not, think about why you still have it as part of your life. Give away or dispose of things that only consume space in your house. Learn to pick and choose what goes into your schedule, only filling it with activities that bring you closer to the things you value most. Most of us need to go through this exercise annually to keep from accumulating things that are of no use to us in our life.

#40 Holiness of the Body

Your body, as a Christian, is the holy vessel God gave you.

A holy creation that carries the indwelling presence of the Holy Spirit. Your body is a gift worthy of life here on earth and for accomplishing what God wants you to do in and through you. It is a reminder of the sanctity and beauty of your life as the child of God. Handle your body in holiness, with respect, since it is to be used to spread the Good News of Christ and in service to others. Appreciate your body's uniqueness as well as its sacredness, since through it you can live on earth the one and only life.

The Big Idea

To the Christian, your body is considered a sacred vessel, a gift from God, a temple of the Holy Spirit. This precious gift enables you to carry out God's will for you here on earth and to show the beauty of holiness in being God's child. Therefore, care for and respect your body, and use it to show expressions of love, acts of kindness, and compassion while enjoying the qualities that make this temple unique and special.

The Word

Romans 12:1-2 *Therefore, I urge you, brothers and sisters, in view of God's mercy, to offer your bodies as a living sacrifice, holy and pleasing to God—this is your true and proper worship. Do not conform to the pattern of this world, but be transformed by the renewing of your mind. Then you will be able to test and approve what God's will is—his good, pleasing and perfect will.*

This Scripture calls us to present our bodies in their entirety to God, not to give in to cultural influences, and to be transformed by His truth in our thinking and life. It is a call to wholistic sanctity-a reminder that all of life, even the health of our bodies, is an act of worship and should reflect our commitment to God.

Putting It Into Practice

Commit every area of your life unto the honor of Christ- even your body. Keep your body as a holy vessel: do nothing that will hurt it, and do things that glorify God, like worship and prayer. Use your physical presence to serve others and share the love of Christ. Whether serving at a community shelter, taking part in the activities at church, or helping a friend in need, follow Jesus' teaching about compassion and kindness. This is the means whereby your body is dedicated to a cause above that of ordinary living. By doing so, you actually live your life as one who bears testimony to your faith in Jesus.

"

Quote: It's never too late to take your health in your own hands and start creating a healthier lifestyle. – unknown

"

Relational Capital

This section focuses on the investment in relational capital. The only things that will last through eternity are relationships: our relationship with God and others. Investments include time, energy, and effort into developing these healthy relationships with family, friends, colleagues, and even strangers. Relationships are integral to who we are as followers of Jesus. Nurturing the relationships we have with others pays dividends not only in emotional comfort and a sense of belonging but also in modeling God's love and grace to a world in desperate need of it. Gaps in our relationships can be mended, unity fostered, through intentional acts of kindness, empathy, and forgiveness as we model Christ's teaching in our daily lives. It is, ultimately, an investment in relational capital, the actualization of God's love in the lives of people, through relationships rather than as a form of personal gain or social influence.

#41 Relational Evangelism

The last words of Jesus are to be some of the most important directives for us as Christians. Sharing the gospel with others is vital to living a purposeful and intentional life as a Christian. We are called to emulate Jesus' footsteps to spread His message of salvation to all nations for the fulfillment of the Great Commission. We have the opportunity to participate in God's mission. Sharing the Gospel is a demonstration of your love and care for others; it is a presentation of hope, forgiveness, and eternal life through belief in Jesus Christ. We are driven by deep care for others. As we share the Gospel in a manner sensitive to and respectful of others, we are actively participating in God's work, making a change in the lives of all with whom you share.

The Big Idea

Evangelizing or spreading the Gospel is one way to live an intentional life. We share Jesus because we care about other people's spiritual well-being. Such kingdom work gives us satisfaction as we take part in something that positively contributes to building God's kingdom here on earth.

The Word

Colossians 4:3 *At the same time, pray also for us, that God may open to us a door for the word, to declare the mystery of Christ, on account of which I am in prison.*

Paul is asking for prayer that God would give him an opportunity to share the Gospel even while in prison. This verse gives insight into the role of prayer regarding the sharing of the Gospel as we seek guidance and intervention from God in opening the doors for us to proclaim the message of Christ. May we pray in this way for the Lord to open doors and use us!

Putting It Into Practice

One practical way you can apply sharing the Gospel in your daily life is by initiating conversations in your relationships and watch for opportunities to share your faith in a natural, respectful way. Examples of this may be inviting friends to church events, sharing your testimony, having deep discussions about faith, or simply modeling Christ's love and compassion in every interaction. But you can have an effective sharing of the gospel, and an awesome impact on the people in your life, by just being intentional and prayerful.

#42 Investing in Relationships

To build and deepen relationships each of us has to invest time, energy, and be intentional. Having deliberate conversations, building trust, and sharing experiences helps to establish significant relationships. Through the intentional formation of meaningful connections, lives can be changed for the good, growth can happen, and individuals can experience the deep love of Christ through such a priceless investment. By focusing on relational capital, we are able to love others as Christ has loved us. We demonstrate His compassion, allow others to experience Christian community, and help develop others in their discipleship journey.

The Big Idea

Investing time, energy, and intentionality in building relationships is vital for fostering meaningful connections and personal growth. By prioritizing trust, communication, and shared experiences, individuals can experience the transformative power of Christ's love in their relationships.

The Word

Romans 12:4-5 *For as in one body we have many members, and the members do not all have the same function, so we, though many, are one body in Christ, and individually members one of another.*

This scripture reminds us of the unity and community we have within the body of Christ. Our body has many different parts with differing functions, so too does each individual within the Christian community have a specific function that must be fulfilled. We are called into harmony with one another to work, realizing interdependence on the members who make up the one body.

Putting It Into Practice

One practical way you invest in relationships is by setting aside regular time for deep, meaningful conversations with friends and family. Whether that is a weekly coffee date or a call scheduled, this blocks out time to connect on a personal level and mutually support one another. Another effective method is to make your involvement with community or church groups active-where you can meet new people and also get involved in activities together. It broadens not only your circle of friends, but it also opens opportunities to practice serving and contributing to a community-a sense of belonging and shared purpose.

"

The greatest gift you can give someone is your time, because you're giving them something you can never get back. –unknown

"

#43 Fellowship

Fellowship is a vital part of the intentional Christian life because it puts you with a supportive community of believers capable of offering encouragement, guidance, or even prayer. Our faith grows as we surround ourselves with people who are thinking on the same wavelength as this may give you much-needed support especially during difficult periods of your life. Fellowship develops a sense of community, spiritual development, and the capability to serve together. You can be a blessing to others as you actively participate in fellowship with others. Gathering with others who follow Jesus helps you to stay connected within the church universal as you interact with others who are also on the discipleship journey with you.

The Big Idea

It is, of course, important for the committed Christian to have fellowship as we practice the intentional lifestyle by providing connections with other supportive, believing friends. Participating in fellowship with fellow believers is fundamental for spiritual growth, community, and support.

By surrounding ourselves with like-minded individuals and actively engaging in fellowship, we can strengthen our faith and journey together in discipleship.

The Word

Acts 2:42 *They devoted themselves to the apostles' teaching and to fellowship, to the breaking of bread and to prayer.*

This verse emphasizes the importance of fellowship in the early church, highlighting how believers were committed to learning, sharing meals, and praying together. It teaches us that fellowship is not just a social gathering but a dedicated commitment to community, spiritual growth, and mutual support.

Putting It Into Practice

Experience the joy of being with others in fellowshipping and participating actively in a small group, Bible study, or support group in a church. As you meet together with fellow believers regularly, you can pray, study, eat, and encourage each other and be there through all of life's celebrations and challenges. Make this a priority by implementing fellowship into the rhythm of your life. Through it you will strengthen your faith, deepen your relationships, and live out your Christian Walk intentionally and purposefully.

#44 Encouragement

Encouragement plays an important and necessary role in living a purposeful life as a Christian for many reasons. Encouragement adds to your faith because it reminds you of the promises and faithfulness of God, especially during times of discouragement. It gives you courage to move forward in faith in Christ. It allows you to rise above the challenge because it supports and reminds you about who you are and your identity in Christ. Encouragement creates community, brings growth and accountability within the church, and allows you to be that iron that sharpens iron in proclaiming the Gospel.

The Big Idea

Encouragement is also necessary for Christians to keep their faith strong by reminding them of God's consistent promises. It comforts during times of persecution, stabilizes us in our Christian Walk, and develops endurance for the journey we call life.

The Word

Philemon 1:7 *Your love has given me great joy and encouragement, because you, brother, have refreshed the hearts of the Lord's people.*

This scripture reminds us how fundamentally important encouragement is within the community of Christians. Encouraging and supporting one another as believers is indispensable to bring joy and encouragement to our brothers and sisters in Christ.

Putting It Into Practice

An effective and practical way to encourage people in your life is actually listening to them. Take some time to know what they are going through, showing them that you truly care about their feelings. That alone can go a long way, just sorting out their spirits, and being a sounding board.

Note of encouragement through 'snail mail' is a powerful way to give a friend a boost for their day! Who wouldn't rather get a hand written note rather than a bill in their mailbox?

#45 Moral Support

Giving moral support to people around us is one of the most valued things in living out your faith. As we show compassion and empathy to all, we are planting seeds of support in the lives of other people. This support will not only display the fruits of the Spirit but will also build a sense of community within the life of others. When giving moral support, you are uplifting people around you, comforting them when in need, and giving guidance. With these open armed actions, you are not only showing your faith but showing that you care for others' well-being.

The Big Idea

Providing moral support through compassion and empathy is essential in living out our faith and building a sense of community. By uplifting, comforting, and guiding others, we demonstrate our faith and show that we care for their well-being.

The Word

Galatians 6:2 *Carry each other's burdens, and in this way you will fulfill the law of Christ.*

This scripture focuses our attention to assist one another in their needs. We are called to come alongside our brothers and sisters in Christ to help them with their burdens, comfort them, and guide them. As we help others with their burdens, we will be fulfilling His great command to love one another even as Christ loved us. This reminds us that the body of Christ is interrelated and interconnected.

Putting It Into Practice

An example of this principle applied in daily life would be to contact a friend who is going through tough times and offer a listening ear, prayer, and practical help. When we seek active ways to lift up and support, it is showing the love of Christ as relationships within our Christian community become stronger. It may be regular visits, supportive words, organizing help with daily needs, or simply being there. Such actions are concrete ways of putting your faith into practice in very ordinary and practical ways.

#46 Marriage

Marriage is a sacred covenant, designed by God for life. As we invest in this most holy union, we align with God's purposes for marriage and the family. As we make this relationship secondary only behind our relationship with God, we are demonstrating the love that Christ has for His church. We reflect the picture of love, forgiveness, and grace Christ has shown us. Strong marriages provide a strong, stable environment to raise a family. This bond of love, respect, and support is an example to your children to emulate, providing a strong foundation for generations to come.

The Big Idea

Marriage is a sacred covenant designed by God for a lifelong commitment, reflecting the love and grace of Christ. Strong marriages not only provide stability for families but also serve as a model of love and support for future generations.

The Word

Genesis 2:24 *That is why a man leaves his father and mother and is united to his wife, and they become one flesh.*

This scripture really captures the unity and oneness that marriage brings. It speaks to leaving a previous family unit for the purpose of starting a new family with their spouse. That unity is not just expressed on a physical level but emotionally, spiritually, and relationally. The two become one in every aspect of their life.

Putting It Into Practice

Take time to spend with your spouse. Alone time together will demonstrate how important this relationship is to both of your and it will be an example to not only your children but also to others as you prioritize time spent together apart from the rest of your family. As you give priority to your marriage above any other relationship you protect this precious time with each other. Setting aside time for open and honest communication as well as praying together will build your spiritual commitment, too. This time apart can look like a date night each week or a weekend away together each quarter. The key is to prioritize your marriage by planning time together, just the two of you.

#47 Nurturing Home

Setting up a nurturing home is of importance because it is through it that the home Christ's love is shown to both those who live there and others that come to visit. In creating a nurturing home, you provide a safe environment for your family in which they experience the unconditional love of God. It's your opportunity to build a firm spiritual foundation and help your family grow in the Lord. It's in a healthy home where deep relationships can be built and God's Word shared through intentional discipleship. It is in the home where significant conversations on faith can help all family members to grow in their relationship to God. Such discussions allow for open dialogue, healthy conflict resolution, and a growing understanding of what it means to be family can blossom.

The Big Idea

It is important to create a loving home as a way of living your Christian faith, where your family can experience God's love in their daily interactions. A home that fosters spiritual growth through faith-based conversations, scripture, and other activities helps support spiritual development.

The Word

Psalm 127:1 *Unless the Lord builds the house, the builders labor in vain. Unless the Lord watches over the city, the guards stand watch in vain.*

This verse brings us back to reality: that, without the guidance of the Lord and His presence in our lives, we cannot build a truly nurturing home. We look to God to be the foundation in the home so that He may guide us in our relations and decisions. Where God is invited to the center of our families, we can trust in His provision and protection. As we let God guide us in building and keeping our home, it becomes a haven of peace, love, and growth.

Putting It Into Practice

One way you develop a nurturing home in daily living is by starting your day off with family prayer and devotional time. This sets the tone for the day, enabling God to guide your thoughts, words, and actions. The family is bonded together and supported through actively listening, showing empathy, and expressing appreciation to one another.

"

Real love is about being selfless and giving your all to someone without expecting anything in return. – Unknown

"

#48 Giving Gifts

Sharing your gifts as a Christian is essential for nurturing relationships within the church community. Too often we only think about tangible gifts when we consider giving gifts. Remember that there are so many intangible gifts as well. Recognizing that all gifts come from God, sharing your talents and resources demonstrates a commitment to serving and loving others. This act of giving creates a sense of unity and support as each individual contributes their unique gifts to edify and strengthen the community of believers.

Big Idea

Sharing gifts with each other helps us establish a relationship with others within the community of Christ. You recognize that everything good in your life is from God; you then take your talents and possessions and use them to glorify Him by serving others. This exchange of gifts not only brings stability to each of individual but it will also be one of many avenues to demonstrate unity and caring in the church.

The Word

Romans 12:13 *Share with the Lord's people who are in need. Practice hospitality.*

In this scripture, Paul calls upon the Roman believers to share with the people in need, showing hospitality. We are challenged to be hospitable to one another in sharing our gifts and resources to bless and nurture each other in their time of need. By sharing, you are not only attending to somebody else's need but also enforcing the spirit of unity and love within the body of Christ.

Putting It Into Practice

Discover a place where you can use the gifts you have been given to serve others. Maybe it's a family in your neighborhood that just welcomed a new baby into their family. It may be something as simple as providing a meal for a family that has one member sick at home, offering to sit for that single mom, or taking the time to listen to a friend facing some kind of challenge. You can actually create in a culture of generosity and love by being very much on the lookout for ways to share your gifts and serve others in very practical ways.

#49 Prayer Partners

Having prayer partners can be not only rewarding but also beneficial in growing your relationships. Prayer partners can give spiritual support, encouragement, and guidance to help you stay on the right track in your walk with Christ. Through it all, they keep you responsible for yourself through accountability-to create discipline and commitment to your focus on your spiritual life. Having a prayer partner can bring unity and fellowship within the Christian community to grow your connection with others. They help you make decisions that are wise and in line with the wisdom of God and help you discern next steps for your life. Prayer partners intercede for you in prayer, asking God to give guidance and blessings.

The Big Idea

Having prayer partners is beneficial for deepening relationships and staying focused on your walk with Christ. They provide spiritual support, encouragement, and accountability, fostering unity and fellowship within the Christian community.

The Word

Matthew 18:19-20 *Again, truly I tell you that if two of you on earth agree about anything they ask for, it will be done for them by my Father in heaven. For where two or three gather in my name, there am I with them.*

This scripture illustrates the power of agreement in prayer, the promise of Jesus' presence when believers come together in His name. This brings into focus the unity and fellowship that must accompany prayer, coupled with the assurance of God's faithfulness in answering the prayers of His children.

Putting It Into Practice

Engage regularly with a small prayer team composed of a few close friends or some family relations. If your church doesn't have a prayer team, create one. You may meet regularly, sharing needs with which to be in prayer, interceding for each other, studying the Bible together, and encouraging one another in living purposefully for Christ. Having prayer partners keeps us accountable to the discipline of having a life of prayer.

"

An unintentional life accepts everything and does nothing. An intentional life embraces only the things that will add to the mission of significance. -John Maxwell

"

#50 Be a Mentor

Developing mentoring relationships is significant for individuals seeking to be purpose-driven. A mentor provides valuable spiritual guidance, illuminating Christian values and biblical truths to help strengthen your relationship with God. This journey is not just about gaining personal insight; it is centered around discipleship and being held accountable. Your mentor walks alongside you, ensuring that your actions align with the teachings of Jesus and encouraging you to make faith-based choices each day. However, this process also allows for personal growth. Mentors assist in recognizing and utilizing your unique talents for the greater good, fostering both personal and spiritual advancement. During life's challenges, your mentor offers emotional support and moral advice, helping you stay grounded in Christian beliefs. The true beauty of this experience lies in the opportunity to eventually mentor others, passing on the torch of faith and intentional living to create a lasting legacy. Find a mentor and then begin to think about who you can mentor.

The Big Idea

Developing mentorship relationships is essential for those seeking a purpose-driven Christian lifestyle, as mentors provide spiritual guidance and support to help individuals grow in their faith and personal development. Through this journey of discipleship and accountability, individuals are prepared to pass on their knowledge and faith to guide others in perpetuating a legacy of intentional living.

The Word

Proverbs 27:17 *As iron sharpens iron, so one person sharpens another.*

This scripture has perfectly captured the meaning of Christian mentorship. It is a Godly call in mutual growth and edification in the body of Christ. Even as iron sharpens iron, our faith and character are refined in interaction with fellow believers. A mentor not only shares his or her wisdom but also learns and enlarges through the relationship-this in itself is a process of mutual sharpening to our potential.

Putting It Into Practice

Being a mentor may look as simple as a weekly coffee with someone looking to use the opportunity as a tool for discipleship. You may spend time in prayer together, sharing what you're learning from Scripture, or simply encouraging one another. If someone is struggling with a working decision, then you as a mentor can help guide them to see what scripture says about the situation. In this way, that decision can be aligned with God's Word. It is this kind of regular, intentional interaction that not only keeps us in step with God but also develops strong relationships within the body of Christ-living out the reality of "iron sharpening iron" in practical and effective ways.

#51 Find a Mentor

Receiving mentorship is significant in your own Christian journey. A mentor not only offers guidance based on their own spiritual experiences but also provides wisdom to help navigate the complexities of faith. This relationship involves more than just advice; it includes accountability to uphold Christian values and promote consistent faith practices. Additionally, mentorship plays a vital role in your discipleship, nurturing a deeper understanding of the Bible, enhancing prayer effectiveness, and fostering spiritual discipline. It encompasses a comprehensive approach to your spiritual development, addressing various aspects of life through a Christian perspective.

Mentors offer essential support during challenges, providing encouragement, perspective, and a reminder of God's enduring love, strengthening your resilience and perseverance in your spiritual journey.

The Big Idea

Finding a Christian mentor is beneficial for you because through this relationship, it brings guidance, wisdom, and accountability into your life. It will help you have deeper biblical insight, pray effectively, and keep you accountable in the spiritual disciplines. What is more, having a mentor will provide the necessary support when things get tough and to guide you through life's challenges.

The Word

Proverbs 15:22 *Plans fail for lack of counsel, but with many advisers they succeed.*

This verse emphasizes finding wisdom and insight from others. We can see the value of being surrounded by spiritually mature people who can give godly counsel and insight. Just as a multitude of counselors can lead to the success of your plans, a mentoring relationship gives a supportive framework to help you make decisions that are in line with God's will. It speaks volumes about strength found in collective wisdom and a benefit coming from a community with a faith-based grounding.

Putting It Into Practice

Think about individuals in your church who are more spiritually mature than you are. Narrow it down to two or three individuals. Have lunch or a cup of coffee with each of them. Use that time to get to know them better, see if they might be a good spiritual mentor for you, and allow the Holy Spirit to guide you in making a wise decision through this process. We all have seasons in our life where we need a mentor with specific qualities where we need guidance and direction. Having a mentor for your faith doesn't mean that person is with you forever. It may be just for a period of time. After you choose someone, schedule regular times to connect with them to talk about areas in your life where you need wisdom, guidance, and insight.

#52 Reconciliation

As a Jesus follower, we know that we are to forgive others for things that may have happened in the past. We are to make peace and be reconciled to those individuals in our life that have offended or hurt you. Estrangement from those who have wounded us by words or actions will cause you to stay stuck in that anger. Until we are reconciled to the person that we need to forgive or let go of the situation that has harmed you, we will remain trapped. Reconciliation requires that we need to change, bringing personal growth, healing, and a testimony to God's grace. It is a declaration of obedience in spite of our emotions. Only then will we be able to live in peace and forgiveness of the past.

The Big Idea

As followers of Jesus, we are called to forgive and make peace with those who have hurt us. Reconciliation leads to personal growth, healing, and a testament to God's grace, requiring us to change and choose obedience over our emotions, ultimately allowing us to live in peace and forgiveness.

The Word

Colossians 3:13 *Bear with each other and forgive one another if any of you has a grievance against someone. Forgive as the Lord forgave you.*

Paul summarizes Christian living through the act of forgiveness. He calls on us to follow the example of forgiveness that Christ has given us, underscoring that in forgiving, we are not just letting go of something but our desire it to actually pursue peace and reconciliation. The challenge with this scripture is for us to reflect upon the depth of God's grace toward us and to extend that very grace toward one another. This reminds each one of us that, in forgiving, the strength is not from ourselves but in the profound forgiveness given to us through Christ. We are to live in a continuous manner of forgiveness that nurtures reconciliation and healing.

Putting It Into Practice

Think about an individual in your life, either still living or has passed away. Write them a letter pouring out your heart. Spend time with the Lord as you write in order for the Holy Spirit to lead you in your correspondence. You may choose to actually talk with the person who has offended you in order to seek reconciliation. It may be time to take a match to the letter and destroy it. Regardless as to how you are being led, use this exercise to release you from the guilt and shame and allow the Holy Spirit to move you to forgiveness and letting go of the offense. It will change you and eternity because of this healing for your life.

"

The best relationships are the ones where you can be yourself, flaws and all, and still be accepted and loved unconditionally. –Unknown

"

#53 Salt & Light

We are called to be salt and light to this world as a Christian-to be actively involved in your community. Being "salt" means to be the seasoning to keep your community focused on all that is right, true, and honorable. Being the "light" shows your kindness and honesty in pointing others toward the positive influence of Jesus. This role calls us to be deliberate in seeking out how you can make a difference. By intentionally being involved in your community you have the opportunity to carry the banner of Christ and serve others through your witness. Infiltrating neighborhoods, schools, and organizations with your witness for Christ helps to make the world a better place.

The Big Idea

This call to live as salt and light involves the building of bridges to people outside of the faith, reflecting God's love in the ordinary things of every day, and being an influence of hope and light in our world. Not only will this draw people to Christ, but it will also make us more compassionate and understanding on our own journey of faith in Jesus.

The Word

Matthew 5:13-14 *You are the salt of the earth...You are the light of the world. A town built on a hill cannot be hidden.*

This is a call to live for the Lord in such a way that you add flavor and light to life. In just the same way that salt enhances flavor and light dispels darkness, so Christians are commanded to impact the world around them by making God's kingdom visible and tangible to others. Living as salt and light becomes the active expression of Christ, loving and standing as beacons of hope in a seemingly dark world.

Putting It Into Practice

Your call to be the salt and light may be as simple as volunteering at a local food bank, being friendly to the neighbor in need, or faith conversations with coworkers in a manner that is respectful. For instance, you can organize community clean-up days and invite both the church and the locals. This act of service indeed beautifies the community, but it also brings opportunities for relationships and conversations about faith, showing the love and light of Christ through practical and meaningful means. You can be a bright example of your faith, allowing everyone to be given a taste of what God's kingdom is all about.

#54 Relational Evangelism

By investing in the relationships in our life, we are able to build bridges of communication, common experiences, and trust. These bridges can become avenues to share the love of Christ in everyday life. Our call to be the hands and feet of Christ is a testimony to the love and care He gives to His people. Some of the individuals we connect with may not even know Him yet. This provides an opportunity to change someone's destiny in this world and the world to come. Our life becomes an invitation to others to experience God's redemptive love and personally realize life transformation that comes through the Lord. You have been given the gift of participating with the Holy Spirit to bring others to Christ.

The Big Idea

Investing in relationships allows us to share Christ's love, serving as avenues for transformation and offering others the opportunity to experience God's redemptive love. As agents of change, we can invite people to encounter the life-changing love of God through our actions and connections.

The Word

Matthew 28:19-20 *Therefore go and make disciples of all nations, baptizing them in the name of the Father and of the Son and of the Holy Spirit, and teaching them to obey everything I have commanded you. And surely I am with you always, to the very end of the age.*

The command of Jesus summarizes the mission of each believer-to share Christ with others. We are called to actually do more than that. We are to focus on discipleship and teach others to follow the words and ways of Jesus. The message challenges us to be active in the spread and proclamation of the Gospel. We are not alone in doing so; He is with us as we share Jesus with others.

Putting It Into Practice

This one may be a challenge for us. We want to share our story of how your relationship with Christ makes a difference in your life. Take some time to write it out: what was you life like before Jesus? How did He change your life? How do you live out your faith now in everyday life? Practice it in a mirror so you are more comfortable talking with others. Practice with someone from your faith community. This will help you to be ready whenever the Lord opens a door for you to share your faith with another person whether it is in your neighborhood, work, or community.

#55 Gathering with Other Believers

Meeting together with other believers and developing relationships within the Christian community is not just a help, it is foundational to living intentionally as a Christian. You feel a sense of belonging, encouragement, and support that come as you gather with other believers. Fellowship helps brings encouragement and reminds us of our responsibility in living a life according to biblical principles and growing in spiritual maturity. Diversity in the Christian community will develop unity and love of various backgrounds and personality profiles, helping you to understand others better. As you gather with others, you form new relationships within the Christian community. As you expand your circle of friends and acquaintances, you will be able to have a more full and intentional expression of your faith.

The Big Idea

Gathering with other believers is foundational to intentional Christian living, providing encouragement, support, and growth in spiritual maturity. Fellowship fosters unity and understanding across diverse backgrounds, helping you live out your faith more fully and intentionally.

The Word

Hebrews 10:24-25 *And let us consider how we may spur one another on toward love and good deeds, not giving up meeting together, as some are in the habit of doing, but encouraging one another—and all the more as you see the Day approaching.*

This, in fact is a call to frequent fellowship among believers. An appeal to active community, the writer says-a "stimulating of one another to love and good works," not for spiritual health, but to "fellowship." The real coming together in worship is not only a good habit but an integral part of the process of growth that all believers need, in which encouragement plays the central role, especially in the light of the second coming of Christ. It reminds us that our walk by faith is not a solo event; it is intertwined with the welfare and edification of our brothers and sisters in Christ.

Putting It Into Practice

To implement this into your life consider joining a small group of believers or a regularly meeting Bible study. You can go deeper into the Scriptures, share your own insights about the Scriptures, and share both difficulties and successes in life in a close-knit group. Join a church project to serve others or join a ministry team in your church. This allows you not only to contribute your talents and gifts in meaningful service but it also connects you with others who are committed to serving and growing in their faith together. Both practices give you the opportunity to build relationships and live in Christian community.

"

The best way to find yourself is to lose yourself in the service of others. -Mother Teresa

"

#56 Cross Cultural Relationships

Working with people of different cultures and backgrounds widens your scope, influence, and impact in the world. The Great Commission calls you to be part of spreading the Gospel throughout all nations, and to this purpose, you are able to communicate with all kinds of people and spread the love and redemption brought about by Jesus Christ. Meeting others from other regions makes your concept of culture wider, and it increases your appreciation of different types of people. As you begin to broaden your horizons across cultures, you will grow in compassion for others around the globe. It is also a journey to get you out of your comfort zone and expand your personal growth. As you experience multiculturalism you are entering into a rich community to continue to not only build relationships but to help you to better communicate the love of Jesus to others.

The Big Idea

Engaging with people from different cultures expands your perspective, influence, and ability to share the Gospel. It helps you grow in compassion, build relationships, and communicate Christ's love more effectively as you step out of your comfort zone.

The Word

Galatians 3:28 *There is neither Jew nor Greek, there is neither slave nor free, there is no male and female, for you are all one in Christ Jesus.*

This verse captures the heart of Christian unity and identity in Christ. In a world full of partitions and divides, Galatians 3:28 brings us right back to the radical inclusiveness of the Gospel: an announcement that in Christ, cultural backgrounds, races, and skin color is irrelevant. Through Christ, all those who follow Jesus, are include regardless of culture or nationality.

Putting It Into Practice

Intentionally bring together individuals from different cultures. Perhaps this is done through international dinner nights where all people bring a dish from their respective country or culture and allow themselves to learn from each other. Learn about the traditions that are common in their culture and seek to understand more of who they are and how they might celebrate holidays from their perspective. You may even get a taste of what heaven will be like as all who know Him, from all nations and cultures, gather around the throne in worship.

#57 Digital Discipleship

The internet is a tool to be used in the mission field that has totally changed the digital landscape. This great digital frontier means that you have an opportunity for ministry that is unparalleled by any other source, simply because you get to reach people in their quest to know, to connect, and to seek the Lord. The world is literally at your fingertips along with the prospect of bringing individuals from around the world into a relationship with Jesus. Through social media, you can reach, engage, and encourage others in their spiritual Walk with the Lord.

The Big Idea

The internet offers an unprecedented opportunity for ministry by allowing you to reach people worldwide as they seek connection and truth. Through social media, you can engage with individuals and encourage them in their journey with Jesus, making the world your mission field.

The Word

1 Thessalonians 5:11 *Therefore encourage one another and build each other up, just as in fact you are doing.*

This verse invites us into the ministry of encouragement, where positive words and encouragement among believers can make an impact on the lives of others. In the modern day of digitization, the mandate reaches beyond physical gathering to creating a space for encouragement and spiritual growth online. We share hope and messages of encouragement and manifesting Christ's love by making this digital world a place to bring support and hope.

Putting It Into Practice

You can implement digital discipleship by engaging others on social media platforms. Use your Facebook wall or groups to focus on spiritual or ministry interests and share daily devotional content, participate in discussion threads, or offer words of encouragement to people. Use your Instagram or Facebook account to post quotes, Bible verses, or personal reflections that inspire you. Continue posting uplifting and inspiring content to reach more people, and find meaningful connections that cultivate spiritual growth and community building online.

#58 Admitting Wrongs

Probably the most fundamental action a Christian can do is to admit when they've been wrong. As we admit to what we have done wrong, we are able to reflect humility; we are not perfect. We can reflect on our mistakes, learn, and improve through the lessons learned. By practicing repentance and reconciliation with others, we are strengthening our relationship with God. We commit ourselves to living for Christ even when we have fallen short of our intentions. Taking responsibility for wrong actions demonstrates Christ's character and presses you toward humility, accountability, and a continual striving toward Christ-likeness.

The Big Idea

One of the most important actions for a Christian is admitting when they've been wrong, which reflects humility and a commitment to growth. This practice of repentance strengthens your relationship with God, helps you strive toward Christ-likeness, and shows accountability in your walk with Christ.

The Word

Proverbs 28:13 (TLB) *A man who refuses to admit his mistakes can never be successful. But if he confesses and forsakes them, he gets another chance.*

This scripture brings out the transformative power of confession and repentance. It is in harmony with the idea that what spells success with God is not that failure does not occur but is in how we respond to failure. Only through the acknowledgment of wrongs committed can spiritual rejuvenation through God's grace take effect. By confessing our sins, we dedicate ourselves to humbleness and open up our ways to God's redeeming work, clearing the way to true success and prosperity in the Spirit.

Putting It Into Practice

Practice reflective thought as a daily routine for admission to going wrong in some of your relations. That is, regularly take a part of each day over the events of conversations and actions, noticing things that could have been said in a different way. Remember actions that may have been done hastily or incorrectly and check yourself. Think how you may rectify the things that you have noticed. What can you do in order to make right the wrong that has happened?

"

Forgiveness is the final form of love. -Reinhold Niebuhr

"

#59 Holy Spirit Guidance

Inviting the Holy Spirit into the conversations in your relationships is like opening the floodgates for the entry of the Lord's wisdom and guidance. He is considered the third person of the Trinity and can give individual insights from the Lord in your conversations. The Holy Spirit is known as the Counselor and a great help in discerning the situation. Such guidance gives us the ability to have the courage to say what needs to be said in the conversation. The Holy Spirit equips you with the words to say to help you to face those relationship challenges. Wrapped in the grace of the Lord, we will be able to give words of exhortation as we talk with others.

The Big Idea

Inviting the Holy Spirit into your conversations opens the door to God's wisdom and guidance, providing insight and discernment. The Holy Spirit equips you with the right words, helping you face relationship challenges and speak with grace and courage.

The Word

John 14:26 *But the Helper, the Holy Spirit, whom the Father will send in My name, He will teach you all things, and bring to your remembrance all that I have said to you.*

This verse gives us a clear vision of the Holy Spirit as our Helper, sent to teach and remind us of Jesus' teachings. It underlines how He will lead us into all truth, give wisdom, and remind us how Jesus spoke to people, allowing it to be lived out in everyday life. Because the Spirit is always present to guide us regarding God's will, we should not be left to our own decisions in the complexities of life. We seek the guidance of the Holy Spirit in all aspects of our life.

Putting It Into Practice

Practically speaking, asking your relationships to be led by the Holy Spirit may involve stopping to pray for discernment before engaging in those tricky situations or interactions with people. Maybe you need to confront a friend or family member about something disturbing you. Rather than-react, you take a deep breath and silently pray for the Holy Spirit to give you insight into their point of view and the words to bring healing, not hurt. Asking for such guidance of the Spirit may do more than change the dynamic in this interaction; it will grow your dependence on God's wisdom in life's daily conversations and nurture relationships that honor Him.

#60 Encourage One Another

One of the best ways to invest in relationships is to encourage others. As we plant seeds that give those around us courage, we become a beacon of hope to those we come in contact with. It's amazing how one word of encouragement can change a person's whole day. In a world that has so many problems, kind words to others will be a balm to counteract the chaos that surrounds our days. In our interactions with others, encouraging words show that we value them as individuals. We give those we talk to confidence as we encourage them in their day. Although we usually think about such kindnesses when people are going through a difficult period in their life, know that words of encouragement transform an ordinary day into an extraordinary one.

The Big Idea

Encouraging others is one of the best ways to invest in relationships because it lifts them up and shows we care. A simple word of encouragement can turn someone's day around, giving them confidence and reminding them they're valued, even when life's chaotic.

The Word

1 Thessalonians 5:11 *Therefore encourage one another and build each other up, just as in fact you are doing.*

This passage asks us to live as vehicles of encouragement as believers. It congratulates the efforts already done and calls us to continue to build each other up. There are many challenges and discouragements and we are called to bring strength and encouragement to others. In the world around us, there are enough adversaries tearing us down; it's time to build up the body of Christ as we encourage one another.

Putting It Into Practice

Think of someone in your neighborhood, office, or a friend who could use a word of encouragement. Sometimes, just a simple message, or maybe even just a phone call, saying, "How are you?" and "I'll pray for you," does much in the way of encouraging a person. This will show the person that you value them enough to be concerned about them or their situation and that you're willing to support them through your prayers. You might also invite them to be included in your Bible study or small group. This is where insights from Scripture and how it relates to contemporary living are shared, and the level of contact and encouragement goes even a notch higher. Allowing them to feel welcome and heard, you are helping them grow spiritually and get closer to God.

"

A healthy relationship is built on mutual respect, trust, and communication. –Unknown

"

Intellectual Capital

ntellectual capital is the investment we will explore in this section of the book. Intellectual capital dares us to employ our minds and our talents in pursuit of knowledge, wisdom, and betterment of self with the ultimate and major impact on and influence on those around us. We should consider being a good steward of our intellectual gifts and talents as we remember the parable of the talents: using our resources in service of others, knowing that God is thereby glorified. By desiring to learn constantly, by acquiring new skills, and by making use of those in the service of others, we deepened our insights into the world and realize our God-given potential. As we develop our intellectual gifts, our desire is to serve others. We learn and grow so that we are better able to transform dreams into realities. We use our minds to create possibilities of how we might be used by God in service to a particular segment of the world's population. As we pursue excellence through our intellect, we are able to be faithful stewards of the mind that God has given us.

#61 Mentally Equipped

As we equip our minds, we not only engage in understanding but also are equipped for the ministry God has called us to. Through preparation we are able to combine spiritual growth with skills to serve others. We learn and understand God's Word in order to advance the Gospel. We are able to witness in a more compelling manner. We are prepared mentally for meaningful conversations and able to respond to challenges we might face. It is through such equipping we are able to make contributions in the work place as well in the organizations where we are involved. A significant consideration in this regard is how to overcome any preconceived anti-intellectualism among some Christian groups by underlining the fact that attaining real knowledge is in tune with faith in the best sense of a pursuing faith that inquires and comprehends. To put it differently, investing in your intellectual capital has been proven to serve not only your spiritual journey but also build your capacity to manifest your call with conviction and intention.

The Big Idea

Equipping our minds not only strengthens our understanding but also prepares us for the ministry God calls us to. By combining spiritual growth with knowledge, we can witness more effectively, engage in meaningful conversations, and serve with greater conviction and purpose.

The Word

Matthew 22:37 *Jesus replied: 'Love the Lord your God with*

all your heart and with all your soul and with all your mind.'

This is the heart of the Christian message, emphasizing the holistic approach to our faith. To love God with all your mind means to be intellectually engaged with our faith. It means understanding the depths of what God has said and His creation-questioning, exploring, inquiring into it. This is anything but an academic exercise; it's a kind of worship, inasmuch as our striving for the truth brings us closer to the God who is Truth. It invites us out of our comfort zones and into our faith with energy and reflection.

Putting It Into Practice

This can be put into practice by setting time aside each day or week to study the Bible more in-depth on a deeper level, possibly using a commentary or study guide to understand historical context, language, and theology. Find a Bible study group that encourages deeper questions and discussion. You can also read books on Christian apologetics to better equip yourself for faith-related conversations-anticipating and answering questions intelligently and respectfully-in a manner which attracts confidence and respect from others. In so doing, you will grow intellectually while deepening your understanding of God and His world, living out your faith more effectively.

#62 Renewing Your Mind

Renewing your mind is actually intentional Christian living where we in our deepest thoughts, beliefs, and actions are changed to be like Jesus. This renewal of the mind is important as we practice discernment. We are able to understand more of God's will and be empowered as you live out His purpose in the midst of our worldly challenges. Renewing your mind is the process of overcoming harmful patterns that keep us in bondage. It's through plunging into God's Word, opening yourself to guidance from the Holy Spirit, and making you aware of which areas of your life need transformation. Through this ongoing renewing of our mind, we can be transformed into the image of Christ.

The Big Idea

Renewing your mind is an intentional process of becoming more like Jesus in your thoughts, beliefs, and actions. By immersing yourself in God's Word and allowing the Holy Spirit to guide you, you can break free from harmful patterns and better understand God's will, leading to transformation into Christ's image.

The Word

Romans 12:2 *Do not conform to the pattern of this world, but be transformed by the renewing of your mind. Then you will be able to test and approve what God's will is—his good, pleasing, and perfect will.*

This scripture underlines the potency of renewing your mind. The passage contrasts believers from being conformed by worldly patterns to metamorphosing into transformation with a fresh mindset- the mindset of Christ. This is not only discarding worldly values but it involves embracing a style of life that helps you discern and live out God's will. It is by the renewing of your mind that you come into alignment with the will of God for your life, and your life becomes rewarding and a proper reflection of His goodness, pleasing nature, and perfection.

Putting It Into Practice

The realistic and practical way to renew your mind as a Christian is to set aside time each day to be spent in the reading and meditation of the Scripture. These two practices allow you to engage with biblical truth. God's Word orients our thoughts and actions. Add to this practice praying regularly for direction and strength from the Holy Spirit. You will be able to have a deeper connection with God through prayer so that His wisdom impacts your decision-making and steers you through life's complications with a renewed perspective.

"

An investment in knowledge pays the best interest. - Benjamin Franklin

"

#63 Discernment

The practice of discernment will help you align every decision of your life according to your faith and values. This spiritual skill will enable you to navigate life's complexities and make sure your choices reflect God's will. Through the use of discernment, you will avoid many pitfalls of deceptions that happen when people embrace false teaching and ideologies that have taken people away from a biblical path. It is about more than just making good choices; it is about making God-honoring decisions in respect to relationships, careers, finances, and personal development. Discernment also acts as a shield to protect against spiritual assault, temptations, and all the subtleties of spiritual warfare. It equips you with the ability to recognize and resist the schemes of the enemy to stay on course in faith and thus contribute to spiritual well-being. To put it in a nutshell, discernment is the compass that will get someone through life with wisdom and in fidelity to God's kingdom.

The Big Idea

Discernment helps you align your decisions with your faith, ensuring they reflect God's will and protect you from deception. It serves as a spiritual compass, guiding you through life's complexities with wisdom and enabling you to resist temptations and stay true to God's kingdom.

The Word

Philippians 1:10 *so that you may be able to discern what is best and may be pure and blameless for the day of Christ.*

This verse in Philippians summarizes the heart of discernment within the Christian life. Paul prayed for believers to be able to discern what is best, which shows the weight of our choices needing to be in harmony with God's will. Discernment, in this regard, is not aimed at making right from wrong but at recognizing the best and God-honoring course of action in every situation. It means the maturity of faith that enabled believers to live pure and blameless lives.

Putting It Into Practice

Before you make any major decision, you may want to retreat to a quiet place to pray, asking for God's guidance and wisdom. This is especially relevant when a new job is offered to you or another big decision is to be made. But look for discernment not only in the life altering decisions but in the ordinary, daily ones as well. You might get great discernment as you search the scriptures and seeking out the advice of mature believers who can help make your decision.

#64 Christian Meditation

Christian meditation is the use of a passage of scripture to mold your life around the wisdom of God; it means going down to the very heart of Jesus through reading the Word. This practice silences your mind and shifts your attention to the presence of God. It creates a better relationship with Him because you are finally quiet enough to actually listen to Him. It is the journey of developing this spiritual intimacy wherein silence becomes the soil for hearing the whisper of God, guiding you towards His will. But above all, it is more than a personal act of tranquility, but a way of attuning what you are doing, your goals, and priorities to God's purpose. Christian meditation nurtures mindfulness and self-awareness, which is important in dealing with your thoughts and emotions. It helps you to take on a reflective approach to life where every thought and action would be a well-thought step in being conformed to the image of Christ.

The Big Idea

Christian meditation involves reflecting on Scripture to align your life with God's wisdom, fostering spiritual intimacy and attentiveness to His presence. This practice helps you cultivate mindfulness and self-awareness, allowing your thoughts and actions to be guided by God's purpose and conforming you to the image of Christ.

The Word

Psalm 19:14 *Let the words of my mouth and the meditation of my heart be acceptable in your sight, O LORD, my rock and my redeemer.*

This verse is a beautiful encapsulation of the idea of Christian meditation. This becomes a prayer of alignment of our inner reflections and outer expressions to God's will. He prays that 'My words' and my 'thoughts' be acceptable to God. This scripture shows the need for control over our hearts and minds to keep them in line with the mind of God. This reminds us that our meditations are not just for self-improvement but are also an offering pleasing to God.

Putting It Into Practice

One practical way to incorporate Christian meditation into your daily life is to begin by meditating every morning upon the scriptures. Before the demands of the day take hold and get a stranglehold on your agenda, take a few quiet moments to read a passage from the Bible, then sit in silence as the words resound deeply within your heart and mind. Reread the passage slowly three times to get the full expression of the words. Intentionally slow down each verse so that you might grasp the full understanding of what the Lord is showing you through these verses. Reflect on the passage and the application that the scriptures have to your life, and listen for God's guidance as you remain quiet in His presence.

#65 Stewarding Your Life

All we have is a gift. As followers of Jesus, we see our life and all that is in it as a gift from God. While God does entrust these resources to you for your own benefit, He also wants you to use them with wisdom and intentionality. Managing the gifts well reflects your response of gratitude to Him and that you are lining up your will with His. By using your mind in the planning of your life and making decisions that continually reflect your belief, both in life decisions and specific daily activities, you live intentionally. The point here is not personal gain; it is an investment toward a larger vision, incorporating the skillful stewardship of all you have been given to serve God and help other people. In all you do in your life, you should think, plan, and act with intentionality, focusing at all times on the value of your assets and the impact you can make as you steward your life well.

The Big Idea

Everything we have is a gift from God, entrusted to us to use with wisdom and intentionality. Stewarding these gifts well reflects gratitude and aligns our will with His, focusing on serving God and others rather than personal gain, while making thoughtful, faith-driven decisions.

The Word

Psalm 20:4 *May he give you the desire of your heart and make all your plans succeed.*

This verse in Psalm 20 points out the harmony of our desires, plans, and God's will. This is a reminder that when the desires of the heart are in line with the purpose of God, and we plan our lives around these godly aspirations, He supports and blesses our endeavors. It's about syncing our deepest wishes with what we know pleases God-living an intentional life aligned with His divine purpose.

Putting It Into Practice

Take an inventory of all gifts you have been given. It may be a home, a family, a source of income, etc. Make a list. Think about each of these gifts and rate yourself as to how you are stewarding them. What grade would you give yourself in each of these areas? What are some ways to immediately begin to be a better steward of one of the things on your list? Which of them would require a longer-term focus in order to be a better steward? If you begin making changes today, you will begin to implement this practice into your life. Periodically evaluate your life looking at how well you are stewarding different aspects of your life.

#66 Get Wisdom

Living intentionally as a Christian requires more than the heart; it requires an all-out mental engagement in pursuit of knowledge, wisdom, and understanding, especially of the things that are important to the Kingdom. This intellectual engagement is necessary for discerning what is true from what is false as we swim in a sea of diverse ideas, philosophies, and beliefs. Knowledge and insight are so important in helping sift through various perspectives that are presented day by day, and allow you to stand on the solid foundation of Scripture. Participation of your mind enables you to interweave your faith into your daily life. Wisdom and knowledge are not mere concepts but things that give you practical wisdom to make informed decisions, looking at justice with compassion, and applying biblical principles to life regarding personal relationships, professional undertakings, and community involvement. The development of wisdom is definitely not a passive act; it is an active and lifelong pursuit that would touch upon every area of your life.

The Big Idea

Living intentionally as a Christian requires engaging your mind to pursue knowledge and wisdom, especially in matters of the Kingdom. This intellectual pursuit helps you discern truth, apply biblical principles in daily life, and make informed decisions with compassion and justice.

The Word

Proverbs 4:5 *Get wisdom, get understanding; do not forget my words or turn away from them.*

This scripture seeks to illustrate the vital role played by active pursuit of wisdom and understanding that is so central to the Christian Walk. It calls us to prioritize our life on these pursuits, embracing God's Word as the ultimate guide. It is not an endeavor that is passive but rather the conscious choice to accept and live by biblical teaching, realizing well that wisdom and understanding are more than intellectual assets alone: They are spiritual necessities to living, deciding, and interacting with the world around us.

Putting It Into Practice

A practical example of how you could apply the pursuit of

wisdom and insight to your everyday life might be in the context of decision-making on the job. Before any business decision, you stop and reflect on not just the bottom line but, more importantly, if this decision aligns with biblical principles. Ask yourself, "Does this action promote fairness, honesty, respect toward others? In taking this ordered reflective process-by means of pursuit of wisdom and understanding-ensures even within the business world, your actions demonstrate your faith and lead to a life intentionally lived for God.

#67 Engaging Mentally

Engaging your mind builds empathy and compassion, which allows you to actually see and meet needs around you. Your mind helps you make educated, thoughtful decisions for the purpose of serving effectively. In a world full of issues-poverty, injustice, and inequality-applying your critical thinking and problem-solving skills becomes paramount. It is through these efforts-undergirded in prayer and the seeking of divine wisdom-that you affect positive change, manifesting God's love in action. This practice respects your commitment to follow Christ and presses upon you the call to engage your mind on behalf of the world's needs, creatively addressing those needs with mercy and justice. To take on the mind of Jesus in your actions and thoughts, and to use your mind in the service of others, becomes a part of every moment. It is representative of the selflessness and love that Jesus expressed and opens the path to a concerned yet capable ministry. Your mind is challenged to empathize, make righteous choices, and wrestle with some of society's most thorny concerns with biblical insight and thoughtful analysis.

The Big Idea

Engaging your mind fosters empathy and compassion, helping you make thoughtful decisions to serve others effectively in a world filled with challenges. By applying critical thinking and biblical insight, you can address issues like poverty and injustice with mercy and justice, reflecting Christ's selfless love in your actions.

The Word

Romans 12:2 *Do not conform to the pattern of this world, but be transformed by the renewing of your mind. Then you will be able to test and approve what God's will is—his good, pleasing and perfect will.*

The Scripture invites us on a journey of transformation, where our minds are not conformed to this world but are daily renewed by a Christ-centered worldview. It involves testing and approving God's will-testing necessitates an intentional action and adjustment in behavior. It is such renewal that actually empowers one to find his place in God's kingdom and to minister with the gifts and talents He has given to others.

Putting It Into Practice

Intellectual engagement in deciding on your life starts with an immersion into continuous learning. Besides engaging in the study of the scriptures, here are some additional ways to engage your mind intellectually. Read books, attend seminars, and look for educational resources that would give you a broader understanding and insight into different subjects. This will not only equip you with knowledge but also outline ways in which you can think through a problem critically and arrive at a well-informed decision. Another practical way is reflective thinking. Set aside a regular time for personal introspection and prayer concerning events that have occurred, the decisions made, and what happened as a result of those decisions. Reflect on how your decisions are or are not congruent with that which is important to you and to your faith. Pray for the discernment of the Lord to lead and direct you. In addition to on-going learning, reflective practice you will approach decision-making in a manner that creates a sound foundation toward a purposeful and thoughtful process.

#68 Engaging the Culture

For the Christian called to live a purposeful life, engagement with culture is important. It puts us in contact with people of different backgrounds, beliefs, and values and can serve as a backdrop for discussions related to faith. Keeping up with cultural trends is not only about being relevant but also to understand what is taking place within society so that we can best address it from a Christian perspective. The communication of the gospel needs to make sense in a current cultural context. You are called to be the salt and light that advances love, justice, and compassion. By being engaged, you contribute both by words and actions to impact your community.

The Big Idea

Engaging with culture is essential for Christians to

effectively communicate the gospel and address societal issues from a faith-based perspective. By staying informed and involved, you can be a positive influence, sharing love, justice, and compassion through both words and actions.

The Word

Matthew 5:13-16 (NIV) *You are the salt of the earth. But if the salt loses its saltiness, how can it be made salty again? It is no longer good for anything, except to be thrown out and trampled by men. You are the light of the world. A city on a hill cannot be hidden. Neither do people light a lamp and put it under a bowl. Instead, they put it on its stand, and it gives light to everyone in the house. In the same way, let your light shine before men, that they may see your good deeds and praise your Father in heaven.*

In the passage, Jesus applies the metaphors of salt and light to describe the mission-essential role of Christians in the world. Salt is called to enhance and preserve by adding flavor and preventing spoilage; Christians are similarly called to enrich and preserve the goodness in society. Light is indicative of clarity, truth, and guidance; it is symbolic of how believers are called to light up the world with Christ's love and wisdom. This scripture emphasizes that this is not an option but a responsibility to influence the world positively.

Putting It Into Practice

Spend time in the area where you live. You can volunteer to help local non-profits, schools, or community centers take advantage of those opportunities to build relationships and demonstrate Christ's love through serving. Participate in community events that meet local needs or point to local concerns as a natural opportunity to not only know and better understand the culture but to make an impact in it through your service. By the fact that you get involved and become a presence in these places, you are contributing to positive change.

"

Education is the most powerful weapon which you can use to change the world.- Nelson Mandela

"

#69 Transforming Culture

As a Christian, changing the culture involves intellectual engagement as change agents of society. You have the power, by engaging in the world, to challenge and counter the influences in culture that are not healthy for individuals or society. You do this with critical thinking, and by being intentional in your dialogue, you advance the truth of God's Word to keep it central and relevant in a rapidly changing world. As you go about being change agents in culture, you're in a position to shape moral values and principles reflecting biblical emphasis that serve society's constructive interests. You can turn your mind into a useful tool for transforming culture and be proactive in making changes for the betterment of the culture in general.

The Big Idea

As Christians, transforming culture requires intellectual engagement and intentional dialogue to challenge unhealthy societal influences and keep God's truth central.

By actively shaping moral values based on biblical principles, you become change agents, using your mind to positively impact and improve culture.

The Word

2 Corinthians 9:8 *And God is able to bless you abundantly, so that in all things at all times, having all that you need, you will abound in every good work.*

This scripture reminds us that God is able to provide us with everything we need to do good works and to leave a mark in this world. With our dependence on Him and the sharpness of our intellect to transform the culture, He will bless our efforts for effectiveness. As we serve through our good works, we have the opportunity to impact our communities and culture.

Putting It Into Practice

If you are a Christian concerned about changing the culture, there is one active and practical means through which you can bring change, by participating in community outreach and service. In participating in such programs, you get an opportunity to express Christ's love in action and to impact everyday culture with your presence and influence. Be the good in the world in both word and deed. Another practical way is to engage in faith-based dialogues on social media platforms on various spiritual and moral issues. You can have the opportunity to challenge cultural misconceptions and share your biblical perspectives through discussions extending beyond your immediate circle of influence, contributing toward shaping a wider understanding of Christian values through the digital age.

#70 Defending the Faith

Defending your faith with intellectual rigor becomes absolutely necessary as we stand firm in that which has been given to us through the ages; it's a matter not only of obligation but also of heart. Such intellectual defense of faith-apologetics-will enrich your faith by having a critical analysis and understanding of the faith that was once delivered to the saints. Apologetics equips us to share the Gospel in a logical way through meaningful dialogue. Knowing what you believe and why you believe it is significant in your witness to those you meet. Grounding your faith in theology, history, and apologetics will give you not only the confidence to defend your faith but also assurance of the foundation upon which Christianity is built.

The Big Idea

Defending your faith with intellectual rigor, or apologetics, enriches your understanding of Christianity and equips you to share the Gospel logically. Grounding your beliefs in theology, history, and apologetics strengthens both your confidence and your witness to others.

The Word

1 Peter 3:15 *But in your hearts revere Christ as Lord. Always be prepared to give an answer to everyone who asks you to give a reason for the hope that you have.*

This verse calls us to deeply understand our hope in Christ and to prepare ourselves for sharing it whenever asked. It is not to win arguments but to give a mature explanation of the gospel-convinced in truth and love. Grounded in faith, we can engage people on meaningful levels, showing why we believe and live as we do in a humble and kind manner that reflects Christ's character in every interaction.

Putting It Into Practice

Explore some tools to help equip you in Christian apologetics. There are many books that are currently available to help you lay a firm foundation for your faith. Discover a beginners apologetics course online. These resources help you to delve into theology and a greater understanding and knowledge regarding Scripture and Christian doctrine.

#71 Articulating Your Faith

Your intellect plays such a pivotal role in articulating your personal faith journey and in your ability to communicate it clearly. As you map out your own story, you begin to demonstrate to others the difference that Christ has made in your life. Expressing your life before you began to follow Jesus, what happened in your life to begin the Jesus way, and how your life is now. Being ready to tell your own story will not only ground you in your faith but also help you to be ready when you have the opportunity to share your journey with someone. Retelling your own spiritual narrative allows you to plant seed of faith into the lives of others.

The Big Idea

Your intellect is key in articulating your faith journey and communicating it clearly to others. By sharing how Christ has transformed your life, you not only strengthen your own faith but also plant seeds of faith in those who hear your story.

The Word

Matthew 22:37 *Jesus replied: 'Love the Lord your God with all your heart and with all your soul and with all your mind.'*

This is quite a profound Scripture in that it calls us to holistic devotion; it points out the idea of loving God with every part of our being. This invites us to apply our intellect to God's presence in our lives, encouraging the seeking of an understanding, wisdom, and discernment in doing so. Loving God with our mind means being in pursuit-actively-so as to find more knowledge about Him, reflecting upon His Word, and allowing the things one finds to transform life and thoughts. As you do so, you will be able to articulate your faith to others in ordinary ways every day.

Putting It Into Practice

Engage the Scriptures with critical inquiry: ask questions, establish context, and compare interpretations. This can take place through personal study, joining a group for Bible study, and even attending seminars and lectures concerning biblical topics. In so doing, you further your knowledge of the Word of God and prepare yourself for better dissemination of the Gospel, whereby you can state your faith and reasons therefore with clarity and confidence. As you begin to articulate your own story into the larger story of the purposes of God, you will begin to better understand that as believers we are partners in God's great mission here on earth. Once we articulate it, we can share it, we are ready to share it.

#72 Active Learning through Listening

In order to really listen to others and to the Lord, you have to be still. As you practice the spiritual disciplines of silence and solitude, you begin to more clearly understand what has been written in the scriptures. You begin to see how you might apply the principles to your life and to live into your kingdom calling. Listening to others as you build relationships is an important aspect of developing connection. We are too often thinking about what we are going to say next and are not really listening to what the other person is saying. Being present and listening helps us to learn what is actually happening in their life and be able to provide wise counsel in their situation.

The Big Idea

To truly listen to God and others, practicing silence and stillness is essential. By being present and attentive, you gain clearer understanding of Scripture and can offer meaningful connection and wise counsel in relationships.

The Word

John 10:27-28 *My sheep hear my voice, and I know them, and they follow me. I give them eternal life, and they shall never perish; no one will snatch them out of my hand.*

This scripture tells us to pay attention to God's voice in order to have significant development in spiritual growth. It prompts us to increase our knowledge about Jesus Christ and live as He taught. When we increase our knowledge about God and His Word, we get to see not only our personal growth but also glorify God. We are able to follow Him more faithfully. This expansion capacitates us to handle life's situations with poise and wisdom so that at any given time, the life of Christ may be manifested in us.

Putting It Into Practice

One of the most effective ways to listen for and hear God's voice in your life is to make writing out Scripture and journaling a part of your daily rhythm. Set aside a certain time of day for prayer and to write out passages of Scripture. Sometimes, writing the words out can enhance your times of meditation and help you focus entirely on what God might be saying through His Word. Writing slows us down so that we are actually able to learn and comprehend what is being said in God's Word. Build on this practice by keeping a journal where you not only write your prayers but also any kind of insight or message you might feel God is giving you. By keeping a journal, you can track spiritual revelations long-term and get an idea of the direction God might be leading you and how it would go with God's guidance in action.

#73 Discernment in Making Decisions

Whether you are trying to decide who to marry or what job to take, we want to be wise and have discernment in making decisions, especially the big ones. As we evaluate the pros and cons of each situation, we pray for spiritual discernment as well as utilizing our intellectual capital to make the best decision possible. We are to look at the actual facts around the scenario mapping out all that we know about it. Using our minds and not our emotions, keeps us from making major mistakes in our life. Other important considerations are looking to see how the situation aligns with our core values and the other things that are really important to us. Looking to compare and contrast different opportunities helps us to have greater discernment and make wise decisions.

The Big Idea

When making important decisions, we seek wisdom and discernment by evaluating the facts and praying for spiritual guidance. By using our intellect rather than emotions, and aligning choices with our core values, we can make wise, well-informed decisions.

The Word

James 1:5 *If any of you lacks wisdom, you should ask God, who gives generously to all without finding fault, and it will be given to you.*

This is a scripture that impresses the need to seek the Lord's wisdom concerning all situations including the decisions we need to make. It reassures us that in such pursuit, God is ready, willing, liberal in giving, and without reproach wisdom as we may need. A promise like this is one to be cherished in a world where wisdom always appears in scant supply. It calls us to come to God in prayer for the insight and understanding we need to make wise decisions, assuring us that our Heavenly Father is the very source of true wisdom.

Putting It Into Practice

As you have decisions to make, take some time for authentic discernment. To be proactive for important decisions that come along, map out the calling God has on your life. How does this decision impact that calling? Mine your core values. How does this opportunity align with your core values? List out the non-negotiables in your life. What implications would this possibility have in those areas you will not compromise? What about the things you want to do in your life? How does this situation measure up to those? Take time to think through each area of the decision that needs to be made. Discern what is the best direction for you at this time in your life. As you think through these important aspects of your life prior to an actual decision needs to be made, you will be ready have the discernment needed to make a wise decision.

#74 Ethical Decision-making

As we think through the decisions we make, whether in our personal life or business, our desire is to engage your intellect in a purposive-ethical way. That means much more than following the rules; that means discerning how to accomplish the goal God's way. This goes so much further than any form of analysis; this is an engagement in God's purposed will, an integration of head and heart. You weigh options and their potential consequences, seeking to act in ways that will honor God and convey His love. Jesus' command to love God with your heart, soul, and mind, and to love your neighbor as yourself, underpins this journey. It puts the mind in a disposition where love, compassion, and justice flow through it. By being consciously aware of how you use your mind, you will be enabled to live out the life of Christ in you in the middle of complexities and make ethical decisions that echo His desire for humankind.

The Big Idea

When making decisions, whether personal or professional, we should engage our intellect with ethical purpose, aiming to align with God's will. By integrating heart and mind, and seeking to honor God through love, compassion, and justice, we make decisions that reflect Christ's teachings in the midst of life's complexities.

The Word

Micah 6:8 *He has shown you, O mortal, what is good. And what does the LORD require of you? To act justly and to love mercy and to walk humbly with your God.*

This perhaps summarizes the heart of ethical Christian living: a call for justice, mercy, and humility in daily walk with God. To act justly means the making of right and fair decisions, not merely those that benefit us. To love mercy means showing compassion, forgiving, and reflecting God's heart. To walk humbly with God describes living a life submitted to God's guidance, under His sovereignty in all our choices. These principles serve as some kind of associating compass for Christians in making ethical choices pleasing to God and contributing positively to the world.

Putting It Into Practice

Activate this ethics-based, ethical decision-making in your life as a Christian through regular consultation with wise, spiritually mature mentors in conjunction with the principles outlined in scripture. Wise and ethical decisions are made in conjunction with others who have the same framework for their life. Having an accountability group for personal goals with other believers who take ethics-based living as serious as you do. This type of community offers the needed support, insight, and feedback toward decision-making that coincides with Christian ethics and promotes spiritual growth in your life, as well as others around you.

#75 Think Creativity

Looking at the biblical narrative in the book of Genesis, we see the God created. We are not only to be creative but also to use our mind to think creatively. Included in stewarding our life well is the use of our intellectuals and artistic gifts to think and solve problems. Whether it is an artistic endeavor or to think outside of the box in designing solutions at work, we are called to be creative. As we participate in creative works we are reflecting the nature of the creator God as well. Through creativity we not only use our abilities but also our talents to develop plans, ideas, and dreams to bring to fruition the vision that God has for our life.

The Big Idea

In Genesis, we see God as Creator, and we are called to reflect His nature by using our creativity in both artistic and intellectual pursuits. By thinking creatively and solving problems, we steward our gifts and bring God's vision for our lives to fruition.

The Word

Exodus 35:31-33 *He has filled him with the Spirit of God, with wisdom, with understanding, with knowledge and with all kinds of skills—to make artistic designs for work in gold, silver and bronze, to cut and set stones, to work in wood, and to engage in all kinds of crafts.*

This text brings out the fact that God has given His people different talents and gifts, not for personal satisfaction, but for His intention. It basically shows us that creativity is a God-given tool that should serve the community and be to God's glory.

Putting It Into Practice

There are opportunities to serve in ways to let your creative side shine. Your church may have a media team that needs you or perhaps using your artistic skills in community outreach programs. Learning and utilizing tools for graphic designing that can be used to communicate on social media may be a way to exercise your creativity. What about serving on a task force or committee that needs help to strategically plan for the future for a project or ministry area? There are so many possibilities! Pray and ask the Lord to open doors for you to use your creativity to serve in an area in your church or community.

"

The function of education is to teach one to think intensively and to think critically. Intelligence plus character- that is the goal of true education. -Martin Luther King Jr.

"

#76 Pursue Justice

Engaging your mind to gently but unmistakably guide culture toward matters of justice, compassion, and biblical values is important for a number of reasons. As a Christian, we understand that faith without works is dead. In pursing justice, we are putting our faith to work. Considering the needs of our churches, organizations, neighborhoods, and communities, we know that there is a plethora of opportunities to pursue justice. Most societal issues are complex and need to have passionate individuals working on the situation from all fronts to make a major impact. We may not be able to do everything to eradicate the situation but we can do something. Whether we approach homelessness, human trafficking, or drug addiction, we have the opportunity to make a difference in the world.

The Big Idea

Guiding culture toward justice, compassion, and biblical values is essential, as faith without works is dead. While societal issues are complex, Christians can take meaningful steps to address challenges like homelessness or human trafficking, making a positive impact where you can.

The Word

Proverbs 28:5 *Evildoers do not understand what is right, but those who seek the Lord understand it fully.*

This scripture emphasizes the desire for divine wisdom to make known what is right and wrong. In a world where truth and morality often seem gray, availing ourselves of

God and His teaching brings clarity and direction. Our seeking to understand, as believers, through the perspective of God enables us to work out the complexity of culture with justice and compassion, acting in a manner congruent with biblical truths.

Putting It Into Practice

Roll up your sleeves and begin to better understand all of the dynamics involved in whichever area you are passionate about in your community. Volunteer at the local food bank. Serve a meal at the homeless shelter. Find one area in your town or city where justice is lacking and begin there. The opportunities are plentiful and as you take one step into serving, you may discover a greater compassion for those in need.

#77 Broaden Your World

We often stay within our own little bubble and don't go beyond our errands, work, or neighborhood boundaries. Part of investing in intellectual capital is to expand our world whether that means in the city where we live or around the world. Learning about various ministries or nonprofits that serve in various places helps us to get outside of the familiar and broadens our world. We have the opportunity to travel with a purpose whether it's to serve on a mission team or visit historical locations that have had a great impact on Christianity. Having conversations with those who are different from us help to broaden our world as we seek to understand various frames of reference. As we broaden our world, we are opened up to learning more about how we might be able to make an impact through our life.

The Big Idea

We often stay within familiar boundaries, but expanding our world is key to growing intellectually and spiritually. By learning about different ministries, engaging with diverse people, or traveling with purpose, we gain new perspectives and discover ways to make a greater impact in the world.

The Word

Ephesians 4:22-24 *You were taught, with regard to your former way of life, to put off your old self, which is being corrupted by its deceitful desires; to be made new in the attitude of your minds; and to put on the new self, created to be like God in true righteousness and holiness.*

This passage calls believers to transformation through Christ, laying aside old behaviors and thought patterns that are choking spiritual growth. In calling for the renewal of the mind, which is enriched by engagement with diverse disciplines that allow better insight into God's Truth and the world He has created. As we are made new, may we also be open to learning and expanding our vision as we broaden the vision for our life.

Putting It Into Practice

Plan your next vacation adventure with purpose. Research various opportunities to visit the locations where Jesus walked or Paul's missionary journeys. What about a history tour of the reformation or the great revival locations in the world? What about Oberammergau, the passion play that happens only every ten years? There are several organizations that plan such trips for groups and individuals. Learning about these possibilities for this kind of an intentional trip is just a Google search away.

#78 The Next Generation

Living intentionally as a Christian means engaging your mind to train and disciple the next generation. We have a biblical mandate to teach and lead younger followers of Jesus through not only our support but also our mentoring. To guide and instruct those who are younger than we are is one of the greatest intellectual investments we can make. Supporting the next generation through service and ministry within your local church is significant in this great calling of investing in the lives of our younger disciples. We may be planting seeds into their life that we may never see the harvest, yet we are called to pass on the faith that was once delivered to the saints. It's part of being faithful in our calling as followers of Jesus.

The Big Idea

Living intentionally as a Christian involves investing in the next generation by mentoring and discipling younger believers. This is a vital part of our calling, as we pass on the faith and plant seeds that may bear fruit long after we're gone.

The Word

Deuteronomy 6:6-7 *These commandments that I give you today are to be on your hearts. Impress them on your children. Talk about them when you sit at home and when you walk along the road, when you lie down and when you get up.*

This text establishes the necessity of having God's commandments close to our heart and diligently teaching them to the next generation. It reminds us of the need to be discussing these precepts constantly and reflecting upon them throughout daily life, whether at home or on the go, from morning until night. It reminds parents and guardians of our children and youth to teach biblical principles in order to make the faith profound and lasting, it also reminds us that God's teaching should be an underpinning of all life.

Putting It Into Practice

One of the most powerful ways you could apply this scripture to daily living is by holding family devotionals or Bible studies with your family, no matter what age. You could make it as simple as discussing a Bible verse over dinner and asking each person what they think the verse means and how it may pertain to them-perhaps at school or with friends. This allows teaching Christian values to come out naturally in your life and conversation while creating a home atmosphere where the faith you believe in is lived and shared. Live far away from your children or grandchildren? Use the gift of technology to have intentional conversations to pass on the faith to the next generation.

#79 Faith and Science

As a thinking Christian, you know that faith and science go hand in hand. Embracing science is an honor to God since

He has been the ultimate source of all truth, including the laws devised for this physical world. This approach will help you avoid the very common mistake of compartmentalizing faith and science, which may then create conflicts. Integration encourages us to be actively involved in the different scientific spheres for the advancement of medicine, technology, and the care of God's creation. Merging faith with science will enable serving and witnessing to the world even more, showing that faith and reason are complementary, not contradictory, and thus help further meaningful conversations across different belief systems.

The Big Idea

As a Christian, integrating faith and science honors God as the source of all truth and avoids the mistake of compartmentalizing the two. Embracing both allows for meaningful contributions to medicine, technology, and creation care, while demonstrating that faith and reason work together, not in opposition.

The Word

Genesis 1:1 *In the beginning, God created the heavens and the earth.*

This Scripture establishes one important reality: the entire universe is God's work. This is the premise of scientific research. All comes from God including the laws of nature, physics, biology, or chemistry. Each of these reflect the connection between the God who creates and science. Through understanding science, we are made more aware of God's creation.

Putting It Into Practice

One way to put the connection between faith and science into practice is to care for the environment. Beginning the simple habit of recycling products where it is possible, demonstrates how we are to care for the earth that God has so graciously given to us. Going a step further, continue your research to better understand the connection between faith and science. As we look at science as a way to see how God has created our world with such precision, we get a glimpse and begin to comprehend God's created order.

#80 Engaging Your Mind

As we intellectually engage with our faith, we only develop a relationship with God Himself that is not just based on emotion but on truth. A strong and prepared faith has the ability to stand against heresies and untruths, reinforcing your faith spiritually. God has given us a mind to use to contribute our gifts and talents outside as well as inside the church. Too often Christians are seen as irrational, emotional individuals. By engaging our mind, we are thinking through not only what our faith is based upon but why Christianity has stood the test of time through thousands of years. As we develop a comprehensive understanding of our faith, we will be in a position to share the truth of Jesus in a persuasive and thoughtful manner that expands your witness and ministry.

The Big Idea

Engaging intellectually with our faith deepens our relationship with God, grounding it in truth rather than just emotion. A well-prepared, thoughtful faith enables us to defend against falsehoods and share the message of Jesus more persuasively, reinforcing our witness and ministry.

The Word

Philippians 2:5 *In your relationships with one another, have the same mindset as Christ Jesus.*

The text calls Christians to engage their minds in effectively imitating Christ in humility and selflessness. It calls believers through the conscious adoption of the mind of Christ to consider the interests of others as more important than personal interests, which is quite thoughtful in faith. This kind of mental engagement enables believers not only to get closer to God but also to testify to their faith in a rational and orderly manner.

Putting It Into Practice

To challenge your mind, consider the study of Christian apologetics and philosophy. In pursuit of these academic disciplines, we can be equipped to not only understand our faith but to better articulate our beliefs. As you examine your life, think about how you can strengthen the engagement of your intellect. How can you enlist others around you to begin to study together? There is not only accountability through group study but seeing issues and situations through the eyes of others helps to go deeper in your learning and understanding of these subjects.

"

Learning is not attained by chance, it must be sought for with ardor and attended to with diligence. -Abigail Adams

"

Financial Capital

As we begin this section of the book, we will go into how as Christians we look at investing in financial capital. Believers are expected to be good stewards with the resources God has placed in our life. That involves managing our self well, utilizing the finances for the advancement of God's kingdom, and making good things happen in the world. Having grateful and generous attitudes toward money will reap lasting change and eternal rewards from the financial assets we have been entrusted with. Financial capital investments are not about growing our fortunes but about expanding the meaning of our resources to uplift people and causes that we really care about. Whether through charitable giving, supporting the needy, or investing in businesses that reflect our beliefs, we all have a great opportunity to act as agents of transformation in this world. This section offers practical advice and inspiration on how to invest financial capital in such a way that honors God and others are blessed.

#81 God Owns it All

All we have is a gift from God. Our role is to be good stewards of the resources entrusted to us. The Bible teaches stewardship through parables such as the Talents (Matthew 25:14-30) that instruct you to take care of what you have responsibly with purpose. This will apply to all areas of life: time, talents, and treasure. The intentional stewardship practiced will not only honor God but will also model the way of life that is filled with gratitude, responsibility, and foresight. As we emphasize our personal Kingdom Calling, we are intentional that our actions contribute constructively in our community and reflect our faith authentically. With a focus on being intentional in our approach to using all of our resources, we will be able to live a life that is in line with our Kingdom Calling.

The Big Idea

Everything we have is a gift from God, and we are called to be good stewards of those resources. By managing our time, talents, and treasure responsibly, we honor God and live intentionally, reflecting our faith and contributing to our Kingdom Calling.

The Word

Deuteronomy 10:14 *To the Lord your God belong the heavens, even the highest heavens, the earth and everything in it.*

This scripture helps us remember that everything we have is God's, and we are mere stewards of His creation. An acknowledgment of God's ownership in our lives includes the motivation to treat our resources with respect, in such a way as to reflect His glory through our faithful stewardship.

Putting It Into Practice

Practice a mindset of gratitude, where you thank God for everything you've ever been given. It is all from Him. An easy way to implement this in your life is to have a Gratitude Jar. Find a jar and as you think of things for which you are grateful, jot it down on a slip of paper. Add the slip of paper to the jar. Share entries from the Gratitude Jar at dinner as you gather as a family. Having a tough day, pull out a couple of the slips of paper and remember what you are grateful for and remember the giver of all that is good, right, and true.

#82 Financial Investments

When God becomes the center of your financial planning, your decisions become led by prayer and biblical principles, moving you toward investments that will honor Him and give life to others. This takes into consideration the welfare of ministries and causes. In the end, making your faith part of financial planning guides you to be a faithful steward of all that God has entrusted to you. You will begin to live a meaningful life that advances the Kingdom of God. Utilizing biblical principles as you make financial investments, helps us to trust God as the giver. He is the great provider for the needs that we have.

The Big Idea

When God is at the center of your financial planning, your

decisions are guided by prayer and biblical principles, allowing you to honor Him and support meaningful causes. By applying faith to financial stewardship, you trust God as the provider and live a life that advances His Kingdom.

The Word

Proverbs 3:9-10 *Honor the Lord with your wealth, with the first fruits of all your crops; then your barns will be filled to overflowing, and your vats will brim over with new wine.*

This scripture shows that God must be first in our finances. As we return to God the first and best, faith and honor are given to Him. This act of faith commits His blessing and abundance to us, reinforcing the principle stated earlier: God rewards those who are faithful in their stewardship.

Putting It Into Practice

Take some time to review your financial investments. Do some research to be sure that the organizations and companies you are investing in are not only reputable but also reflect your life values. Utilize tools to help you with your investigation. Looking to use biblical principles as a guardrail in helping you to make wise decisions, examine types of businesses you are investing in. Conduct this analysis periodically as organizations do change direction and you will want to be sure you are on track as a faithful financial steward.

#83 It's More Blessed to Give

Generous living involves generous giving as well. This practice of giving outstretches your blessings, which enables you to serve more broadly in the communities in which you reside and beyond. As we seek to bless others, we know and understand that we are trusting in God's provision to meet our needs not our wants. Developing the spiritual habit of giving is to be done regularly, not just here and there. It is a lifestyle that is grace-filled and full of joy. We give because He first gave to us.

The Big Idea

Generous living includes regular, intentional giving, which extends your blessings and allows you to serve more broadly. This lifestyle, rooted in trust in God's provision, is joyful and grace-filled, as we give because He first gave to us.

The Word

Acts 20:35 *In everything I did, I showed you that by this kind of hard work we must help the weak, remembering the words the Lord Jesus himself said: 'It is more blessed to give than to receive.'*

Here is the verse that teaches it is more blessed to give than to receive. From this, the believer learns a lesson in selflessness and generosity since it is an action by Jesus himself. You don't give because you want to satisfy the needs of the people but also for the joy and fulfillment that you derive from giving.

Putting It Into Practice

Think of an individual in your church, neighborhood, or community that is in need. How might you bless them this week? Maybe it's getting the groceries they need but can't afford. Maybe it's stopping at the kids' lemonade stand on a hot summer day and buying the whole pitcher. We are blessed in order to be a blessing to others. How might you do that in a tangible way in the next few days? How would that bring you joy to see how you have blessed them?

"

God is the ultimate provider Lean on Him for financial stability and growth. -Rick Warren

"

#84 Providing for Your Family

The scriptures encourage us to plan wisely for the future so that it meets basic needs-be it food, shelter, or healthcare-for your loved ones. By investing wisely, you not only secure a stable financial base in immediate needs but also your long-term aspirational needs such as education and retirement. The forward thinking required for this reminds us that we are to be concerned with the individuals in our family. We are to care for the basic needs of our family. Learning how to manage money as a family is a very practical way for the whole family to be involved in meeting those needs. Understanding financial management is a valuable lesson for children to learn as they begin to manage their own resources. Keeping out of debt is another way to be faithful in providing for your family. After meeting those needs, we can then begin to look at ways to provide for the future needs. Overall, meeting the needs (not wants) of the family are important as we strive to be faithful stewards of what God has entrusted to us.

The Big Idea

Scripture encourages wise financial planning to meet both immediate and future needs, such as food, shelter, and healthcare for your loved ones. By managing resources carefully, families can stay out of debt, provide for essential needs, and teach children valuable lessons in financial stewardship.

The Word

1 Timothy 5:8 *But if anyone does not provide for his relatives, and especially for members of his household, he has denied the faith and is worse than an unbeliever.*

The scripture underlines the severity of neglect in family provision and its spiritual implications. As Christians, attending to the physical and emotional well-being of the family is not just a social duty but a spiritual obligation; this passage shows the depth of this biblical command.

Putting It Into Practice

If you don't already have one, set up a family budge to monitor and manage the needs of your family. Involve the whole family, including children and youth. They will be well-served to learn faithful financial stewardship at a young age. Develop a plan to meet the future needs of your family as well. Think of the possible needs in the next five to ten years. What practices do you need to begin to implement in order to meet those future needs?

#85 Leaving an Inheritance

Leaving an inheritance as a Christian involves the issues

of stewardship, generosity, and legacy all at once. You actually pass on something more valued than material wealth; this is about passing on spiritual and moral values that enable your future generations to sail successfully through their faith journey. This passing of values and belief is actually building a concrete foundation in the heart of the younger Christians to keep alive and grow the Christian legacy. In offering them help and support financially to meet practical needs, you further enable them to follow their God-given callings more freely without the heavy burden of financial constraint. It has been a good stewardship and culture of generosity for the benefit not only of the individual families but also for the broader community to express Christ-like love and care by leaving an inheritance. Leaving an inheritance, more than anything else, has to do with building a future wherein the Christian values will keep on flourishing and guiding the next generation.

The Big Idea

Leaving an inheritance as a Christian involves more than material wealth; it's about passing on spiritual and moral values to guide future generations in their faith journey. This stewardship, marked by generosity, not only supports their practical needs but also ensures that Christian values continue to flourish and shape their lives.

The Word

Proverbs 13:22 *A good person leaves an inheritance for their children's children, but a sinner's wealth is stored up for the righteous.*

This scripture underlines the virtue of thoughtful, forward-looking generosity. It encourages believers to contemplate the long-term effects of their stewardship. By planning to bless both their children and grandchildren, Christians can spread influence and faith over generations while embedding godliness and prudent stewardship.

Putting It Into Practice

Set up a savings plan intended for future generations or invest in educational funds for your grandchildren. You also need to make sure you instill Christian values through your family's traditions, stories, and experiences in living your faith. For example, you could volunteer together at a local charity or church and thus teach the values of service and generosity. Each one of these pragmatic and spiritual investments paves the way so that the inheritance you leave behind is one of value and valued.

#86 Generous Living

Living intentionally as a Christian includes supporting causes that are charitable and align with Christian values. This, in essence, is a teaching of Jesus Christ through love, compassion, and mercies. Giving generously to whatever cause and supporting the organization that helps people in need is a way of showing your love to your neighbor. This aside, it follows the very core of Christian belief and builds a sense of community and shared responsibility. This means you will be able to impact the world with a practical application of your faith and extend God's kingdom by serving others.

The Big Idea

Living intentionally as a Christian means supporting charitable causes that align with Christian values, reflecting Christ's teachings of love and compassion. By giving generously and helping those in need, you live out your faith in a practical way, impacting the world and extending God's kingdom.

The Word

2 Corinthians 9:12 *For the ministry of this service is not only supplying the needs of the saints but is also overflowing in many thanksgivings to God.*

This scripture establishes that giving is not only to meet physical needs but as an act of worship and to evoke gratitude toward God. It reiterates that generosity serves a dual purpose: it provides the means for fellow believers, while glorifying God in that this giving actually stirs up gratitude.

Putting It Into Practice

One concrete and positive way you can apply this in everyday life is by volunteering at, or making a donation to, a local food bank. This action provides much needed assistance to those who lack the resources and at the same time serves as a personal testimony to living out your faith through service. Every gift, no matter how small it is, gives you the opportunity to express your biblical call to care about others and give thanks with your actions. As you provide to others in tangible ways, you become a living example to your children of the importance of serving and meeting the needs of others.

#87 Tithing

Tithing is an intentional way of living the life of a Christian, where your faith and stewardship are deeply set into a practice that puts God first in your life. This practice is where your obedience to God and trust in His provision is manifested. You are giving a certain percentage of your income to the church and other causes to show that God is the source of all blessings. Not only does such an act fulfill spiritual discipline but it also cements your commitment to the church community and greater humanitarian efforts. In tithing, you show gratitude, worship God, and invest in spreading His love and message to the world. By consistent practice of this discipline of tithing, you also remind yourself that in all things, there must be consideration for God, reinforcing the belief that everything indeed comes from and belongs to God.

The Big Idea

Tithing is a Christian practice that demonstrates obedience to God and trust in His provision by giving a portion of your income to the church and other causes. It expresses gratitude, strengthens your commitment to the faith community, and reinforces the belief that all blessings come from God.

The Word

Genesis 28:20-22 *Then Jacob made a vow, saying, "If God will be with me and will watch over me on this journey I am taking and will give me food to eat and clothes to wear so that I return safely to my father's household, then the*

Lord will be my God and this stone that I have set up as a pillar will be God's house, and of all that you give me I will give you a tenth."

The vow of Jacob to God was one of recognition that He was his supplier if He continued to watch over him on this journey. He committed himself to take a portion from all his blessings and give it back to God, a token of thanksgiving and faithfulness. This, to us, shows that trusting God for our needs, recognizing His provision, and committing to giving back as an act of worship and acknowledgment of His blessings are what should be important to us.

Putting It Into Practice

This might be applied in a real life by having regular automatic contributions to your church, or even some faith-based charity. And the great advantages of this are: it's going to be consistent in your giving, no matter what fluctuating circumstance occurs, and it also helps you budget and plan your money as your tithe is foundational to you. In making our contributions consistent, we are practicing the habit of being persistent in our goal of generous living.

#88 Feed the Poor

Jesus reminds us that we will always have the poor with us. As such, we desire to serve as Christ taught, the basic needs for the less fortunate. Through our efforts to feed the poor, we will help put food, shelter, and clean water in front of those in need for an opportunity of survival. By being attentive to the major areas of care, we address not only the immediate, physical needs but also the opening of doors toward spiritual nourishment and community building. A commitment to this service in stewardship of the poor helps reinforces Christian values and increases your impact in the world.

The Big Idea

Jesus reminds us that the poor will always be with us, calling us to serve their basic needs as He taught. By addressing immediate physical needs like food, shelter, and clean water, we also create opportunities for spiritual growth and community building, reflecting Christian values and increasing our impact in the world.

The Word

Matthew 25:35 *For I was hungry and you gave me something to eat, I was thirsty and you gave me something to drink, I was a stranger and you invited me in.*

It is this scripture that challenges us that our service for the needy amounts to direct service for Christ Himself. It challenges us in embracing generosity and hospitality because when we serve the least of these, it is as if we are giving to Him.

Putting It Into Practice

Choose a nonprofit organization in your community that helps to meet the needs of the less fortunate. How might you serve them? It may be to give away some of the clothes from your overcrowded closet. It may be to serve a meal at your local homeless shelter. It may look like collecting canned goods for a neighborhood foodbank. Choose a place to make a tangible investment that will meet the needs of the poor in your community or around the world. In all of these ways, you can live out your faith in concrete and meaningful ways.

"

God's grace can turn your financial struggles into opportunities for growth and blessing. Trust in Him. - Bobbie Houston

"

#89 Financial Responsibility

Being financially responsible with good resource management is important to you and your overall approach to stewarding your life. Good administration is reflected through the wise use of God's gifts in your life. You can, through prudent budgeting, further missions, aid local projects in their needs, and be able to take care of the indigent-to show God's love and spread His message in very practical ways. Besides all this, good financial stewardship means your personal stability will enable you, for the most part, to get involved in more effective ministry and service. It is foundational in carrying out the call God has given us and maximizing your potential as a leader in His Kingdom.

The Big Idea

Being financially responsible is key to stewarding your life and using God's gifts wisely. Through good resource management, you can support missions, help those in need, and maintain personal stability, allowing for greater involvement in ministry and maximizing your potential as a leader in God's Kingdom.

The Word

Deuteronomy 8:18 *But remember the Lord your God, for it is he who gives you the ability to produce wealth, and so confirms his covenant, which he swore to your ancestors, as it is today.*

This reminds us that the ability to create wealth comes from God but also our financial blessings are part of His covenant promise. This is a call to acknowledge God with honor by living a responsible financial stewardship that wisely utilizes resources for a purpose. This verse can inspire us to choose integrity as we handle His finances. It is reflective of God's provision and faithfulness in our life, as that enables us to support His work and help others.

Putting It Into Practice

Being financially responsible involves being content for what we do have. Make a list of all of the things for which you are grateful. What role does the practice of contentment play in your list? As you make you list, what is the difference between what you need to live and what you want? We are most content when we have an attitude of gratitude for what we already have. Practicing contentment helps us to focus on what we already have and keeps us from the idolatry of coveting more.

#90 Biblical Economics

You cannot help but take part in economic activities if you are going to focus on living intentionally and advancing God's kingdom. Your contribution to the economic sphere funds missions, seeks justice, and pursues business ethics. As much as it will support charitable organizations and help the poor, it will also give an opportunity to influence your place of work and marketplace. The integrity, honesty, and equity you show in economic dealings is to show values derived from the Gospel. Afterall, we live in the world where commerce is a part of everyday life, so it is important that we have a biblical approach as we conduct business.

The Big Idea

Engaging in economic activities is essential for living intentionally and advancing God's kingdom by funding missions and promoting justice. By demonstrating integrity, honesty, and equity in your business dealings, you reflect Gospel values while influencing your workplace and the marketplace for Christ.

The Word

Psalm 24:1 *The earth is the Lord's, and everything in it, the world, and all who live in it.*

This reminds us that God is the owner of all creation and its bounty, which he entrusted to humankind to manage. Christians are called to manage such resources not simply for their own benefit but as stewards who deploy God's wealth for advancing the concerns of His Kingdom. If everything we have is seen to be a gift from God, then we will also be more likely to treat our economic activity with the respect and care this trust requires.

Putting It Into Practice

Although you may not be a business manager or owner,

practically all of us pay others for services rendered. Examine your approach to paying for a service and how you might bless others through giving a tip. Or maybe you are a manager and have the opportunity to advocate for better wages for the employees you oversee. How might you put into practice fair and equable wages to others? Use the same question to think about those you might pay to perform maintenance services at your home. By thinking about these labor considerations, the lives of these individuals are not only enriched, but God's love and care are extended further by this practical action.

#91 Blessed to be a Blessing

Funding mission work to share the Gospel is compelling as we strive to let others know of His sacrifice for us. Your giving makes not only the expansion of God's Kingdom further but also your personal relationship with Jesus Christ deeper. We have been blessed so that we can be a blessing to others. The growth of His Church is counting on this kind of generosity in order to share Jesus in the world. Missionary work involves engaging with cultures and global communities through very practical actions: educating and providing health among others. By engaging in such actions, the immediate needs of society are being provided for. It is through such blessings we are able to make a difference in many lives through funding the work of Christ.

The Big Idea

Funding mission work helps expand God's Kingdom and deepens your personal relationship with Christ, allowing you to be a blessing to others. By supporting missionary efforts, you contribute to both sharing the Gospel and meeting practical needs like education and healthcare, making a meaningful impact in global communities.

The Word

Genesis 12:2-3 *I will make you into a great nation, and I will bless you; I will make your name great, and you will be a blessing. I will bless those who bless you, and whoever curses you I will curse; and all peoples on earth will be blessed through you.*

In these verses, God promises Abraham that not only will He bless him personally but through him, all the nations of the world will also be blessed. This covenant reveals an awesome responsibility and privilege for the Christian-to be conduits of God's blessings. Mission work funding is directly about extending those blessings in line with God's plans to reach every corner of the earth with the message of the Gospel.

Putting It Into Practice

It is practical to show that you have been blessed to be a blessing to others, by giving of your time and skills to local community projects. This can be expressed in many forms, such as through: mentorship to the youth, participation in food drives, cleaning in the community, and giving to mission work or charities that provide educational and health resources. Your involvement, and financial contribution, not only meet immediate needs but also establish long-term relationships, make your community stronger, extend God's love and compassion, and profoundly change lives.

"

We can possess nothing—no property and no person...It is God who owns everything, and we are but stewards of His property during the brief time we are on earth. - Billy Graham

"

#92 Funding Missions

Financially funding ministries that serve the basic needs of others, including sharing of the Gospel, is especially significant as a follower of Jesus. By funding mission work and missionaries, you will be in partnership to make Christ known in the world. Whether it is a local, national, or global ministry you help support financially, you are making an eternal investment in the lives of individuals, families, and communities. As investors in kingdom purposes, we will be contributing to both the spiritual and physical needs of those the organization serves.

The Big Idea

Financially supporting ministries that meet both physical and spiritual needs is a vital part of following Jesus. By funding mission work, you partner in making Christ known and make an eternal investment in the lives of individuals, families, and communities.

The Word

Matthew 28:19-20 *Therefore go and make disciples of all nations, baptizing them in the name of the Father and of the Son and of the Holy Spirit, and teaching them to obey everything I have commanded you. And surely I am with you always, to the very end of the age.*

These verses are often called the Great Commission and sum up the missionary mandate given to Christians. It brings into view the call to spread the teachings of Jesus throughout the world, not as an order but as a partnership with Christ, who promises His presence until the very end of the age.

Putting It Into Practice

You could play an active role in mission work not only through financial support but also through frequent prayers for missionaries, missions organizations, and their outreach programs. Your persistent prayers give the critical spiritual support needed to help sustain them in difficult environments and circumstances. You join forces and help create a prayerful environment of support and funding for furthering the Kingdom of God-so the Great Commission may be fulfilled worldwide.

#93 Invest in Learning

Financial investment in education is a critical necessity of living out our purpose. Continuous learning is how we learn to serve others in more efficient and effective ways. Through education we are equipped to expand our reach through both insight and analysis. As we grow in our professional career, we have the opportunity to hold more influential positions which gives us the capacity to have a greater impact on the lives of others. With these investments in learning, you will answer the call to be a faithful steward, leader, and servant in the location where God has placed you.

The Big Idea

Investing in education is essential to fulfilling our purpose, as it equips us to serve others more effectively. As we grow professionally and gain influence, we can make a greater impact, becoming faithful stewards and leaders in the places God has called us to.

The Word

Proverbs 1:7 *The fear of the Lord is the beginning of knowledge; fools despise wisdom and instruction.*

It is this scripture that brings into view the belief that true wisdom begins with the fear of God. Education pursued with this type of reverence turns knowledge into a powerful tool for service and leadership. The pursuit of knowledge, he says, is to be coupled with a humble and teachable spirit, recognizing that all wisdom comes from God.

Putting It Into Practice

Besides looking at your personal budget to see where you can invest in your own education, why not think about how you might impact another individual who would benefit from scholarship sources. Whether it is funding for a short-term mission trip or for an individual working on a degree or certificate, how might an investment in someone's educational endeavors influence the world for the Kingdom? If it is beyond your own personal capacity financially, support someone together as a group.

#94 Impact the World

Utilize your investment of financial capital to become a change agent for Christ in your community and world. Such a commitment to utilize your financial resources helps to fulfill God's unique purpose for your life, develop your capabilities to influence, and empower your servant leadership skills to make a difference in society. By such purposeful and intentional growth, you can be the light on the hill and show the transformative effect that faith in Jesus Christ should have in a person's personal and professional life. Your commitment will inspire others to pursue their God-given callings, developing a Christ-centered community through service, compassion, and impactful change. And you can have the opportunity to impact the world through such wise and intentional financial investments.

The Big Idea

Using your financial resources intentionally allows you to become a change agent for Christ in your community and the world, fulfilling God's purpose for your life. By making wise investments, you can inspire others to pursue their callings and create a Christ-centered community through service, compassion, and transformative leadership.

The Word

1 Peter 4:10 *Each of you should use whatever gift you have received to serve others, as faithful stewards of God's grace in its various forms.*

This scripture brings into focus the Christian's responsibility to exercise God-given talents in service toward others, serving as vessels of God's grace. Invest in personal development as a way to impact others and be faithful in stewarding your life. As we do so, our gifts are honed and put to work in an effective manner for the benefit of others and will have an impact in the world.

Putting It Into Practice

One way to impact the world and be a change agent is to train leaders. You don't have to be in a high-powered position to be a leader who trains other leaders. There are leaders in every area of an organization. Whether have the opportunity to hold training seminars, teach a class, or mentor someone, you have the opportunity to influence other leaders. By utilizing your financial resources to invest in training other leaders, you are multiplying your investment exponentially.

"

You need to treat your finances as a resource God has provided to fulfill your vision, not a tool to fill your life with luxuries. - Myles Munroe

"

#95 Business Investments

Living intentionally as a Christian means financial investments should be placed in companies and ventures that have sound, ethical standards. This is a commitment to stewardship, responsible use of resources, and the fostering of values such as justice, integrity, and care for creation. These investments offer more than financial returns; they contribute to a larger mission of impacting communities and society in a positive way. As you consider businesses to invest in, think about how investing in small companies would help to create jobs in a community, help to bring ethical organizations into the marketplace, and support local cooperation in building thriving populations.

The Big Idea

Living intentionally as a Christian means making financial investments in companies with sound, ethical standards that align with values like justice and integrity. These investments not only offer financial returns but also contribute to positive societal impact by supporting ethical businesses, creating jobs, and fostering thriving communities.

The Word

Proverbs 16:3 *Commit to the Lord whatever you do, and he will establish your plans.*

This scripture highlights that all human activities, including economic business-related ones, must be committed to God. By committing all our plans and investments to God, we submit our efforts to the Lord, looking for all of our activities to be not only profitable but blessed by the Lord.

Putting It Into Practice

As you invest in businesses, do your research to see what kind of company it actually is. How does it align with your values? How does it impact the community? What kinds of standards does it hold? What leadership characteristics does the senior level officers have? Are they individuals of high ethics and character traits? What kind of a reputation does the company have? How do they handle environmental responsibility? Overall, do your due diligence and homework as you make business decisions in which companies you choose to invest in.

#96 Role Model in Financial Matters

Being a model to others in financial stewardship will serve as an example to others. As we make intentional decisions regarding our financial choices, we would help individuals as we provide advice and wise counsel. It would especially benefit those who are younger than we are in order to guide the next generation in financial matters. As managers of money, we choose to align our choices to the values and causes that honor God. As individuals practice responsible, honest, and ethical handling of finances, we provide an example for others to follow. In doing so, we help new investors through being a faithful, focused, and intentional role model to emulate.

The Big Idea

Being a model of financial stewardship sets an example for others, especially the younger generation, by offering wise counsel and guidance. By aligning financial decisions with values that honor God and practicing responsible money management, we inspire others to follow in making ethical and intentional financial choices.

The Word

Titus 2:7-8 *Show yourself in all respects to be a model of good works, and in your teaching show integrity, dignity, and sound speech that cannot be condemned, so that an opponent may be put to shame, having nothing evil to say about us.*

This scripture calls us to be exemplary in our behavior, and that includes our financial dealings. As little as it may seem, our actions and decisions as Christians are to reflect the integrity and dignity as seen in the scriptures. In so doing, we strengthen our testimony while discouraging any criticism from those who seek to disparage our faith.

Putting It Into Practice

Think of someone who may be in your church, community, neighborhood, or a business acquaintance that may be a role model for you in gaining wisdom in handling finances. In the same light, discover an individual who you can help as they learn to navigate how to make wise and deliberate business choices. Find a mentor and be a mentor. This way you will be blessed to be a blessing to someone else.

#97 Having a Will

As a faithful steward of all that God has entrusted to us, making a legally sound will is one of the most important ones. A will ensures that your assets are distributed according to your wishes. Without a will, your assets may not be distributed as you desire; this might set a stage for confusion and possible conflicts among family members or friends. Long-term financial planning includes writing a will that allows you to make decisions on how to handle your assets and liabilities after your passing. You may choose to give significantly to charitable causes and missions through intentional estate planning. Such financial gifts can make a huge difference in the world for the sake of the Kingdom. You have the opportunity to leave a financial legacy that reflects your faith and values as well as lives on beyond your life.

The Big Idea

Creating a legally sound will is a vital part of faithful stewardship, ensuring your assets are distributed according to your wishes and avoiding potential conflict. Through intentional estate planning, you can leave a financial legacy that reflects your faith, supports charitable causes, and continues to impact the world for God's Kingdom.

The Word

Proverbs 13:22 *A good person leaves an inheritance for their children's children, but a sinner's wealth is stored up for the righteous.*

This Scripture brings out the prudent management of finances and moral obligation to transcend immediate needs. The believers are to be faithful in resource management are encouraged to benefit future generations as have a deep commitment to family and community, resonating with biblical values of foresight and responsibility.

Putting It Into Practice

Consult a wills and estate attorney. Although you may have created a will in the past, be sure that it is up to date with any new legal rulings that may have been implemented since the original one was done. After creating your will, place the will in a safe location such as a locked filing cabinet or safety deposit box in the bank when you are done with it. It will save some headaches and frustration later on to know that your family knows that you have a will and where it is. You can leave a copy with others you trust: a family member, or your attorney. In this way, the whereabouts of your will are made known to your family, and they are in an easier position to carry out your wishes without all the panic and confusion that happens after someone passes.

#98 Radical Generosity

Radical generosity exemplifies the very core values of the Christian faith. We acknowledge God as the ultimate giver not only because of Christ's sacrifice on the cross for us but for all that we have been given. All that we have is from God and we can be generous with the resources entrusted to us. Through radical generosity, we acknowledge that we can be charitable because we know that our provision comes from Him. Not only is selfless giving a sign of our dependence on God the ultimate giver but we do so with joy. As we practice extravagant giving, we are moving in ways that are beyond what is typically expected. We want to lavishly demonstrate our commitment to the ways of the Lord through kindnesses to others through radical generosity.

The Big Idea

Radical generosity reflects the core of Christian faith, recognizing God as the ultimate giver and joyfully sharing the resources He's entrusted to us. By giving selflessly and extravagantly, we demonstrate our dependence on God and our commitment to His ways, going beyond what is typically expected to bless others.

The Word

Acts 20:35 *In all things I have shown you that by working hard in this way we must help the weak and remember the words of the Lord Jesus, how he himself said, 'It is more blessed to give than to receive.'*

This scripture underlines the importance of being supportive to those in need and we are blessed through our giving. It encourages Christians to work diligently and give selflessly, knowing that true fulfillment and joy are found not in accumulation but in the very art of giving.

Putting It Into Practice

Add a simple rhythm to your life by thinking of one person to radically bless each week. It may be that you pay for a stranger's coffee at the drive through. It may be to drop of groceries on the porch of a shut in from your church. It may be leaving a tip for your waiter equal to the amount of the bill. Putting this into practice anonymously will add even a greater blessing to your life.

"

Do all the good you can, by all the means you can, in all the ways you can, in all the places you can, at all the times you can, to all the people you can, as long as you ever can. - John Wesley

"

#99 Invest Locally

When we invest in and buy from local businesses, we are not just making a purchase but actually making the community stronger. We are called to love our neighbors and one way to do that is by supporting local businesses. Local businesses rely on patronage in their community just to survive and thrive. By investing your money in the local economy, you are creating jobs, improving families, building it as a community. Many business owners invest their return into people through the sponsorship of local charities and participation in local events. Your investment in them becomes a virtuous cycle of generosity and growth to all concerned. The simple act of putting your finances into action in your community comes more alive with the support of local businesses.

The Big Idea

Investing in and buying from local businesses strengthens the community, creating jobs and supporting families. This act of supporting local economies fosters a virtuous cycle of generosity, where business owners often give back through charitable efforts and community involvement, benefiting everyone.

The Word

Deuteronomy 8:18 *But remember the Lord your God, for it is he who gives you the ability to produce wealth, and so confirms his covenant, which he swore to your ancestors, as it is today.*

This scripture reminds us of the origin of our wealth generation as coming from God. It is a call to recognize

God's hand at work in whatever economic success comes our way and to invest whatever resources He gives us in ways that glorify Him and further His purposes. A proper understanding of our gift for creating wealth can come from God, whereby how we invest in our community ensures our economic endeavors reflect our spiritual engagement.

Putting It Into Practice

To support local businesses, decide to patronize a small store instead of the large chains. An example could be buying from a local, family-owned grocery store or dining out at a local restaurant; this keeps the money circulating within the community, supporting local jobs, and economic development. Christians can become mentors to young entrepreneurs by advising and mentoring them in ways their success would increase the economic base of the community even more, and demonstrate care and concern for the local economy at the same time.

#100 Proactive Finances

Being proactive with your finances is not optional for us as a Christians. The Bible presents all resources as God's provision to us and counsels us to implement wise management of these gifts, especially financial. This will include avoiding unnecessary debt and making wise decisions that honor God's mandate for stewardship. In a world that places material accumulation above most priorities, being proactive in our finances helps us to learn contentment for what we do have. It minimizes frivolous expenditure, living life in a much less complicated and more meaningful way. Good financial planning sees us through and prepares us for possible future demands and emergencies.

The Big Idea

As Christians, proactive financial management is essential, recognizing all resources as God's provision and honoring Him through wise stewardship. By avoiding unnecessary debt and embracing contentment, we simplify life, reduce frivolous spending, and prepare for future needs and emergencies.

The Word

1 Chronicles 29:12-14 *Wealth and honor come from you; you are the ruler of all things. In your hands are strength and power to exalt and give strength to all. Now, our God, we give you thanks, and praise your glorious name. But who am I, and who are my people, that we should be able to give as generously as this? Everything comes from you, and we have given you only what comes from your hand.*

This establishes that whatever possession you have, we are to know that it all comes from God. It underlines the fact that we are mere custodians of His wealth and recognizes that our ability to give is also a talent given by Him. The true spirit of humility, which should be epitomized in the realization that whatever we give, we give back to God. As we emulate Him, we put into practice the habit to foster generosity and good financial stewardship.

Putting It Into Practice

Take inventory of your personal accounts, tracking income and expenses to evaluate your own use of your finances. You will have a realistic picture of what you actually have and make better decisions to be proactive for your financial future. As you examine your accounts, are they in line with your values? How are you practicing saving in order to be prepared for financial emergencies? What contingency plans do you have in place to mitigate times of hardship? How might you change your financial focus to look into the needs you will have in the future? Spend some time reflecting on your current and future financial plans and adjust as needed to be ready for the future needs of your family.

#101 Intentional Investments

As a Christian committed to intentional living, your aim is for every day to count through investing holistically across the five capitals: spiritual, physical, relational, intellectual, and financial. Through this holistic practice, there's an assurance of growth in all aspects of life. The deepening of your spiritual faith through prayer, worship, or scripture study orients and anchors this journey. Physically, maintaining health through exercise, nutrition, and rest enables active service. Relationally, building strong relationships through love, forgiveness, and encouragement demonstrates Christ's love. Intellectually, a lifelong learning mindset and wisdom-producing desires will increase your knowledge and impact. Financially, wise stewardship and generosity will grow your capacity to bless others. By investing in all these areas, you'll be accomplishing your purposes from God every day, making the greatest possible difference in the world.

The Big Idea

As a Christian committed to intentional living, investing holistically across spiritual, physical, relational, intellectual, and financial areas ensures growth in all aspects of life. By nurturing your faith, health, relationships, knowledge, and financial stewardship, you fulfill God's purpose and make a meaningful impact in the world each day.

The Word

Matthew 25:14-30 *Again, it will be like a man going on a journey, who called his servants and entrusted his wealth to them. To one he gave five bags of gold, to another two bags, and to another one bag, each according to his ability. Then he went on his journey. The man who had received five bags of gold went at once and put his money to work and gained five bags more. So also, the one with two bags of gold gained two more. But the man who had received one bag went off, dug a hole in the ground and hid his master's money.*

After a long time the master of those servants returned and settled accounts with them. The man who had received five bags of gold brought the other five. 'Master,' he said, 'you entrusted me with five bags of gold. See, I have gained five more.'

His master replied, 'Well done, good and faithful servant! You have been faithful with a few things; I will put you in charge of many things. Come and share your master's happiness!'

The man with two bags of gold also came. 'Master,' he said, 'you entrusted me with two bags of gold; see, I have gained two more.'

His master replied, 'Well done, good and faithful servant! You have been faithful with a few things; I will put you in charge of many things. Come and share your master's happiness!'

Then the man who had received one bag of gold came. 'Master,' he said, 'I knew that you are a hard man, harvesting where you have not sown and gathering where you have not scattered seed. So I was afraid and went out and hid your gold in the ground. See, here is what belongs to you.'

His master replied, 'You wicked, lazy servant! So you knew that I harvest where I have not sown and gather where I have not scattered seed? Well then, you should have put my money on deposit with the bankers, so that when I returned I would have received it back with interest.

'So take the bag of gold from him and give it to the one who has ten bags. For whoever has will be given more, and they will have an abundance. Whoever does not have, even what they have will be taken from them. And throw that worthless servant outside, into the darkness, where there will be weeping and gnashing of teeth.'

Jesus uses the gold or sometimes referred to as "talents" to illustrate investments in the Kingdom of Heaven. In this passage, a man entrusts his wealth to three servants before leaving on a journey. He gave five bags of gold to one, two to another, and one to the third, each according to their ability. The first two servants invested and doubled their money while the third hid his in the ground. Then, when he returns, the lord rewards those two first servants for their faithfulness and gives them even a greater stewardship and rejoicing. It is then that the master would reprimand the third because of his laziness and fear, taking the one bag of gold, this servant had away from him and giving it to the first. The lord then casts the unfaithful servant into outer darkness where there will be weeping and gnashing of teeth. This parable instructs us to use the talents or resources given by God faithfully and wisely to the Glory of His Kingdom.

Putting It Into Practice

You have been entrusted with and called to faithfulness and wisdom regarding all of the talents and resources God has given to you. Each individual is called to be found faithful in what we have been given. As we invest our gives in ways that honor Him through serving others, we will be able to come before the King and hear Him say, "Well done, good and faithful servant." Pray for the Lord to open opportunities for you so that the Kingdom will be expanded and you are able to be a shining light to the world.

"

When I stand before God at the end of my life, I would hope that I would not have a single bit of talent left and could say: I used everything you gave me. - Erma Bombeck

"

About the Author

D r. Elaine Friedrich is an accomplished educator and leader with a rich background in education, organizational management, and leadership development across non-profit and for-profit sectors. She holds a Ph.D. in Higher Education from the University of North Texas, an M.A. in Christian Education from Asbury Theological Seminary, and a B.S. in Secondary Teaching from Texas Tech University.

Dr. Friedrich's career includes significant roles in local church ministry in congregations from 900-12,000 members. She has also served in various administrative capacities at Strayer University, including Senior Vice Provost, Vice President, and Campus Dean. As a faculty member, she has taught courses ranging from organizational behavior to art and literature at Strayer University, Crichton College, and Memphis Theological Seminary, including internationally at the Methodist seminary in Costa Rica and Brazil.

In addition to her educational roles, Dr. Friedrich is the founder of the School of Intentional Living, hosting seminars, workshops, and coaching to individuals and organizations focused on living each day on purpose.

www.schoolofintentionalliving.com